M000076591

EATING
WITH MY
MOUTH
OPEN

Sam van Zweden is a Melbourne-based writer interested in memory, mental health and the body. Her writing has appeared in the *Saturday Paper*, *Meanjin*, *The Big Issue*, *The Lifted Brow*, *Cordite*, the *Sydney Review of Books*, The Wheeler Centre and others. *Eating with My Mouth Open* won the 2019 *KYD* Unpublished Manuscript Award. Her work has been shortlisted for the Scribe Nonfiction Prize for Young Writers, the Lifted Brow and RMIT non/fictionLab Prize for Experimental Non-Fiction, and the Lord Mayor's Creative Writing Awards.

'*Eating with My Mouth Open* feels like being gifted the most glorious odd-box from the Farmers' Market: inside are delicious, unnameable fruits and shining vegetables. Van Zweden's writing is at once both nourishing and thorny, generous and eclectic, sumptuous and piquant. This book marks the arrival of a fresh voice in Australian nonfiction.'

REBECCA GIGGS

'*Eating with My Mouth Open* is a beautiful book: heartfelt, intelligent and full of love. It is an examination of the complexities of food and the body, their respective cultures, and the ways in which these basic elements inflect and impact upon so many aspects of our broader lives. Van Zweden's curiosity and warmth animate her writing, which is insightful and lyrical, and a joy to read. This is an important book, and one that will have an impact on many peoples' lives.'

FIONA WRIGHT

'A love letter to *Gezellig*, to Dutch comfort, *Eating with My Mouth Open* is a tribute to the rituals of family-making through food. In this excruciating time of bougie food-for-cultural-capital, of "body-positive" rah-rah, of food-loving, body-shaming confusion, Sam van Zweden cuts through the bullshit, arguing that food is for love, and that if we love food, we must love the bodies that food nurtures. Van Zweden is a masterful caretaker of the bodies that have been left out.'

ELLENA SAVAGE

'Sam van Zweden's exploration of the interplay between food and pleasure, guilt and shame, the body in space, time and in all its glory, can be read like a novel – or as a collection of essays – a well-researched degustation of ideas that give us a front-row seat to her "Journey" towards being unapologetically comfortable in her skin. Something we can all relate to.'

ALICE ZASLAVSKY

'This is writing as sustenance. The book's moments of deep insight and intimacy, all its quiet revolutions, are answerable – as is the case with the most enduring nonfiction – to two gods only: truth and nurture.'
MARIA TUMARKIN

'*Eating with My Mouth Open* is beautiful. Sam is an incredible writer and is amazingly attuned to those tender points where food tangles with family, trauma, illness and mental wellbeing – she describes everyday food moments with clarity and compassion in a way that made me fall in love with food all over again. It's a wonderful book.'
RUBY TANDOH

'An unsparingly honest self-examination of the hungers, the memories and searingly painful truths held deep within our bodies, and how we may permit ourselves to stop and listen to our bodies, and with this seemingly-simple act, connect the nourishment and care of our physical selves with that of our minds and of our loved ones. Wise and brave and deeply empathic.'
KATE RICHARDS

'Absolutely the best kind of memoir: enthralling, empathic and empowering. A beautiful and important book to read at a single sitting and then return to again and again for the insights it offers.'
DONNA LEE BRIEN

'*Eating with My Mouth Open* is a warm and thoughtful contemplation of what it means to have a body, to eat, to grow, and to feel like you are too much in a society that rewards thinness and smallness, especially in women. It investigates the way that attitudes towards food are ingrained through culture, family, and memory, for better or worse. Both deeply personal and thoroughly researched, this intimately written book contributes to the conversation regarding diet culture and body acceptance in fresh and thought-provoking ways. Van Zweden is a conscientious and generous writer, whose words will resonate greatly with anyone who has ever felt uncomfortable in their own skin.'
ELOISE GRILLS

'I sensed that it was connected to the taste of the tea and the cake, but it went infinitely far beyond it ... It is clear that the truth I am seeking is not in the drink, but in me.'
— *Marcel Proust*

'... like most other humans, I am hungry. But there is more than that.'
— *MFK Fisher*

EATING WITH MY MOUTH OPEN

SAM VAN ZWEDEN

NEWSOUTH

A NewSouth book

Published by
NewSouth Publishing
University of New South Wales Press Ltd
University of New South Wales
Sydney NSW 2052
AUSTRALIA
newsouthpublishing.com

© Sam van Zweden 2021
First published 2021

10 9 8 7 6 5 4 3 2 1

This book is copyright. Apart from any fair dealing for the purpose of private
study, research, criticism or review, as permitted under the *Copyright Act*,
no part of this book may be reproduced by any process without written
permission. Inquiries should be addressed to the publisher.

A catalogue record for this
book is available from the
National Library of Australia

ISBN: 9781742236988 (paperback)
          9781742244914 (ebook)
          9781742249438 (ePDF)

Design Josephine Pajor-Markus
Cover design Lisa White
Cover images Stocksy & Shutterstock
Printer Griffin Press

All reasonable efforts were taken to obtain permission to use copyright material
reproduced in this book, but in some cases copyright could not be traced. The
author welcomes information in this regard.

This book is printed on paper using fibre supplied from plantation or
ainably managed forests.

ook was written on the unceded lands of the Wurundjeri people of the
tion.

ntent note: This book includes sensitive material including
isordered eating, self-harm, suicide and mental health. Please
as you need to. Support service contacts are available at the
page 222).

Contents

1

'Your little bottoms', called the dance teacher, 'are lovely peaches!'

When I was very young, from about three or four years old, I took dance classes. Having broken my leg and spent time in a plaster cast, I was too afraid to use it properly again when the plaster was removed. My parents enrolled me in dance classes in the hope that I'd forget the break, or at least become braver in my movement.

I remember raising my arms to reach the barre. I held on tight and inspected myself in the mirror. The barre stretched all the way around the room, with mirrored walls behind.

We were to squeeze those precious peaches as we raised slowly up on the toes of our soft shoes, then lowered back down.

'Look yourself in the eye and say with me – "I. Am. Be-aut-i-ful!"'

At three years old, I didn't doubt it for a second.

Where does that self go? That tiny self with the precious peach bottom, who is unafraid of her own body, and who believes she is beautiful. Where does she evaporate to? Because I find it hard to believe she's still inside me.

Now, as an adult, my body moves so differently. I feel

unable to look in the mirror and repeat the mantra, but some days I can feel those soft shoes back on my feet, and test out what it feels like to raise my body up and lower it back down. I feel the rippling in my calf muscles, the clench in my hips. I explore the boundaries of what my body can do.

Somewhere in between these two awarenesses of my body, I came to see it only as a liability. For the longest time, its tender edges pressed against the world and hurt: against clothes; against those who love it; against perception and choice; against enjoyment. My body's unbearable influence on my experience of the world became too much of a ruling force for me to ignore, and so I needed to get to the work of unpacking my shame and fear. I needed to understand my unassuageable hunger. I make it sound direct – it was not direct.

This isn't a recovery story – God, I'm so weary of recovery stories. I'm tired of 'the journey'. In my own experience, things sometimes get better, or they change shape, but they aren't *fixed*. Fixed would mean I could turn my back on it and move on. I cannot. Things *have* changed, and maybe this movement implies a journey, but 'journey' brings with it a suggested destination. I haven't *arrived*, nor do I expect to.

Essayist and poet Fiona Wright writes of recovery: 'There's no room in any narrative of recovery I've ever seen for this terrible sadness, this unreasonable fear, and these unmeasurable movements, backwards and forwards and sideways, towards, away from and around whatever a return to health might mean'.

This is not a recovery story. Perhaps it's a love story instead.

2

Here's how this book used to start:

My father was a chef for twenty-five years. My mother is morbidly obese.

These are perhaps the most factual statements I can make. They're not tainted by my worldview, or the love I feel for my parents; these two facts exist and are true. Independent of me, or life, or anything else.

I am the daughter of two people who inhabit these two states, and I struggle to know what this means. My own relationship with food feels like a knot that is worth unpicking, or is at least worth the attempt. The not-knowing is a fact as real as the others.

When I wrote this beginning, I didn't yet know. I didn't yet understand. All I was aware of was the worrying fray that tore at my insides. Shame kept me anchored and immovable – fearful – but I didn't have language for that just yet.

Even so, the desire to apologise is strong.

Moving towards the discomfort, I can only whisper *I'm sorry, I'm sorry.* I write towards the apology.

This is how this book used to start, and so much has changed in the writing.

I fear that I've written us into a corner already.

3

Some octopuses bite off their own limbs. Scientists don't really know why. The missing limbs were first thought to be an act of 'autotomy', like when lizards drop their tails and grow new ones. In the case of the octopuses, though, they sometimes pull their arms off as an act of intimidation during fights, or as part of an impressive mating ritual. Octopuses breed violently, holding their potentially cannibalistic partner at a distance for fear that their little deaths might become big ones.

There are octopuses that do this out of excessive stress or boredom. And there are those whose nervous systems suffer from infections, that, for some reason, need those limbs to be gone. Severing a part to save the whole. But this doesn't account for all the missing limbs.

The creature's posture shifts – they hold the offending arm as close to their mouth as their anatomy will allow, and eventually bite. They chew and gnaw until the body part is separated. I don't know if it bleeds. I imagine squid ink in water, but red.

It's called 'autophagy' – self-eating. But although they bite these limbs off, they're not intended as a food source. The octopuses often don't eat their severed limbs at all; their mouths are simply the weapons by which they separate themselves from themselves. Or perhaps their mouths are the tools by which they restore balance to their bodies, continuing on one limb fewer, having done what was required.

—

I grew up by the ocean. Memories from early in my life and the experiences that shaped who I am today are surrounded by trees – the confetti of acacia, and the unblinking eyes of banksia, and the thin paper bark of melaleuca. In my mental landscape, there are swooping birds, and a seasonal tourism industry's clip-on koala souvenirs and fairy penguin keychains.

Phillip Island's tiny off-season community was safe, and close, and known. Everyone was someone's relative, or a family friend, or worked at someone's mate's take-away shop. Small communities are intricate webs in that way. The island's finitude made it an unthreatening community, which I later understood as a difficult place to have any secrets or privacy, and finally – when school was done, and I considered myself grown – a good place to leave.

That first move: bookshelf and bed, guitar and amp (to raise my voice, because then I had so very much voice), my medications and CDs and journals. There wasn't much more. All of these things fit into Dad's small car and a trailer, and he drove me the hour and a half from our old home to my new one. The roads got wider; we swung around the huge roundabout that has since been bypassed, and it slingshot us towards the city. Alongside the road, the dry grass and coastline turned to suburbs and traffic.

Neither of us spoke.

The year or two leading to this young adult freedom was tumultuous. My anger, my rage; the overwhelm of the world, and all of my emotion against it; my inability to name my feelings, or move or change or coax or dress them up or kill them; my muteness and my incredible volume. At some point in my mid-teens, the existence of all these things inside of me became apparent, and they imploded, together, all at once. Folding inward, I began to self-harm. I stole box cutters from the supermarket where I worked, and from my father's toolbox, and wore long sleeves and pants around my family. I didn't understand it then, and I still – more than fifteen years later – don't quite know what to make of it now. But this is the part of myself I recognise in the octopus – the inexplicable need to destroy the body as some kind of protest against all the things that cannot be stopped. The damage that feels more acceptable than the alternative distress.

It was a lot at the time, and it remains a lot in my memory. So much so that I can't explain it chronologically, because the causation is too tangled, and to do so would require far too much going back. That's not this project. Starting to explain one thing, I realise it needs to come later – forgive me, it's incomplete. Instead, I recall it as a series of moments. Out of order; it's a whirlpool of memory. And there's a lot here, so it's okay if you don't catch it all, but let's take a swish around in those moments anyway.

Visiting Mum's new apartment, just a few streets away, I assess the beige carpet, the bare walls, the too-heavy curtains – I can't deal with this. I can't add this to all the unfamiliar things in my life right now; I just need to get through the last year of school in one piece. Looking at Mum, I think *She's okay, she'll be okay*, and return to the familiar house only half believing this. Later I find out again and again all the ways in which she was not okay and I chose not to stay.

With both my parents in the lounge room, just before they separate – or maybe after they get back together for a short time, before parting again – I have been crying and feel newly light, because the unsayable thing and the imprecise words I use are something like, 'I'm bisexual, I like girls *and* boys'. I want for just a moment to shove the words back into my mouth, but Dad responds: 'It can be Prince Charming, or it can be Princess Charming riding in on their horse, I don't mind. As long as it's not the horse'.

People at school are less kind about my coming out.

About once a week, Mum and I sit on the spare bed in her craft room, and we play at pattern-matching. We're trying out blocks in varying stages of becoming a quilt called 'Crazy Hearts'. It's made of clashing colours, and the material has been sourced from Mum's craft room, and from people who love me – friends and family, and friends who are like family. It's silent there too; the only noise is my jeans swiping against her polyester crepe trousers as one of us leans forward to move a patch. Moving one patch causes a chain reaction, and the colours surprise us again. An unexpected partnership between orange confetti and mauve stripes is pleasing, but leaves us with blue and green (without the requisite *in between*). We keep shuffling the patches.

My self-harm escalates until I no longer feel I have other options, and one day – seemingly, just like that – I wake up in hospital after an overdose. It's not the only time; there are more attempts in the years that follow, and I now can't even remember what it was about. But that's always been the problem – getting to the point where it seems like nothing is *about* anything. After the high school attempt, I sleep with the weight of my quilt over the top of the hospital blanket pressing down on me, pushing all the raging static energy in my body back together. When I wake, I'm told that a friend carried me from the school library to the nurse's office, and that I arrived here in an ambulance. I wonder whether he found me heavy. I don't remember any of it. When I leave the hospital with my parents (having added to their already considerable pile of worries, and mostly oblivious to how tender this must make them feel), there are just so many more unsayable things.

There are other hospital visits in that period, not my own. Mum and Dad are both unwell – Dad with depression, which keeps him isolated and internal, smoking in darkened rooms, angry as hell, and when that gets as bad as it can get, he has a heart attack (just like that). It's unsurprising, given this whole whirlpool situation, but it surprises me anyway. Mum's unwell with schizoaffective disorder, which one doctor describes to me as sitting somewhere between bipolar and schizophrenia.

I struggle to tell my friends all that's happening at home, and I start laughing or keeping my mouth shut because it feels too absurd to explain. Instead, I drink on the weekends. I hitchhike along the highway between towns in my area. I sleep in a football ground scoreboard, and leave in a fit of giggles with my best friend when we wake to the Sunday morning match set-up. I cut my hair and dye it, I cut my body and hide it, I start not-eating to see how that feels, and then I start eating again with all the force and space inside of me. There are one or two people I can tell, though, and while they have some distance from the events, they are close to me – they help hold me together. Those friendships are casualties of time, ultimately. They're gone again by the end of high school, because – well. It is a lot.

Somehow I do make it to the end of high school, though. I achieve an average score in the final exams – placing at the lower end of my high-achieving accelerated class – but I have lived through it, and at this time, surviving is the most I can manage. It is the most we all can manage; not just me but my exhausted support network, too. I feel as if I might never stop apologising for that time.

Sometimes my scars take me by surprise – I forget they're a part of my body. This happens with tattoos and birthmarks, too – after some time, these things blend into the body's landscape. The eye doesn't pick them up. But occasionally I remember. And occasionally, I am horrified.

I look in the mirror and I *see* my body, and it does not always feel like my own. Sometimes it feels like war.

—

What goes into my own mouth is dual: it's everything and it's nothing. It is twinned: control and chaos.

Two states: I'm feeling something. I'm feeling nothing.

There are moments where my body and my emotions feel monstrous – where they feel not-my-own.

Fridge. Couch. Fridge, pantry. Fridge.

By the time I'm standing in front of the fridge or pantry, it's too late.

When I used to hurt myself, I was turning parts of the outside world into weapons and marking or opening my body with them. Around the time I stopped, I started eating in more complicated ways. Now my weight fluctuates along with my mental health, and the correlation isn't a simple one in which embodying 'health and fitness' means my mental health is in good shape. At my most slender, I thought about food constantly. Now, I often eat to tamp my feelings down; compacting them inside my insides. Sometimes just being alone and at a loss can be enough for me to seek something to put in my mouth, much like a small child with a pacifier.

At the same time, there's so much joy available in food, too. Cooking (for myself, for people I love) can be one of the most constructive and helpful ways to self-soothe. Slowly stirring a pot on the stove, or letting the house fill floor to ceiling with the heady smell of a winter warming stew, I extend some kindness to myself and find an outlet for creativity that isn't on a page. Sharing a meal can bring me back to my body with a sense of compassion.

But not today. Today is a monstrous body day. A food-as-emotional-compactor day: Load. Gather. Sit. Survey.

Both binge eating and self-harm put me in a place of sensory overload, crowding everything else out. In the white noise of having done either thing, I find relief for a fractional moment – a breath – before guilt creeps in.

Spoon. Open, chew; open, chew. Shove it down.

What I have eaten is messy and incoherent. What I have eaten is out of control. It is mindless and desperate – but having filled every gap inside myself, there's nowhere for anything else to live. No stray feeling can hide, and everything held inside my body becomes written on its outside.

This. This table scattered with packaging and nothing that makes up a proper meal, nothing satisfying, nothing that felt good – this is what I have eaten.

So what am I, having eaten? What *am* I?

—

At my final appointment with the family doctor before I left home, I was told to 'try and lose some weight'. Our family doctor was kind – I remember his skill in explaining complicated medical ideas, his care for each member of our family, with all our associated bodily and mental health concerns. He led me compassionately through my adolescent depression, and oversaw medication changes – most of which carried a warning about weight gain on the in-box leaflet. He was kind in that appointment when he asked me to try.

So when I left home and started out on my own, I tried. I started a soul-crushing job at a call centre, where I met my partner, Danny. He is the good thing – the true and lasting thing – that I have retained from that period of my life. He encouraged me to walk into rooms with my head up, and he continues to do this. His tall body envelops my short one, his cynicism and realism counter my scrambling need to be kind and liked all the time. He takes photos and sees people clearly – we match. He isn't such a big part of this story – the unpicking has not required me to unpick him, or us. We remain intact. He might show up again, though, and I want you to know that he's solid and present even when he isn't mentioned.

'Trying', I walked everywhere, and ate a lot of salads, and counted calories. I bought work-out DVDs and weighed myself daily, recording and worrying over the numbers. I thought a lot – an awful lot – about what was going into my body. I shaped myself into the perfect image of a young woman 'trying'.

I tried to lose weight. I tried to be fit. I tried to do well at my job. I tried to find a place to belong in a new city, with new people. I tried to care for everyone in my life, no matter how far away they lived, and no matter whether I could actually help or control anything. I tried to let go. I tried to stem the panic when I felt it rising in my throat. I tried to breathe. I tried to place my hands on something flat, to remember that I have lived through this before, to put away the familiar thoughts and old habits.

For some time this worked. That is to say, I lost the weight. People commented, telling me that I was a success, and it felt good. I marvelled along with them about how I'd turned things around. I saw myself as a success story; some kind of conqueror.

During one period when the borders of my body became

the most important thing to me, I ran until the numbers on the scale wound backwards, and the expanse of my body magicked itself away. During this time, I ate the foods my body craved – salads and green vegetables – and drank loads of water. Running had made my body bolder in its ability to shout what it wanted, and I became better attuned to hear it. I learned that my body was capable of enforcing change if I pushed it. Running the sloping streets of the inner-Melbourne suburb of Kew, I pushed myself upwards. I listened to my body's every uncomfortable yelp until I reached the top of the suburb's biggest hill, and there, suddenly, was the city. It sprawled and unfolded, the lights winking at me. I was proud of what my body could do. I was someone who ran. I was a runner. I spoke to my body and my body spoke back.

I ran until other people spoke to me about my body, too. Just like they did during my adolescent weight fluctuation, people commented on the change in my weight. They praised my body's new shape and size.

Perhaps it's not where you'd expect, but food memories live in my legs.

In the short-term, eating and running fixed things for me. But long-term, eating and running have not served me.

Eventually, always – another dip in mental health – another medication – another psychologist – another routine – another re-do. Start again. And this time, I must *try*.

—

Dieting can feel like a superpower.

It creates an illusion of control. Dieting makes a body seem, if just for a moment, like a thing that can be manipulated perfectly. This unruly flesh bag becomes an accessory. By restricting and recording, by exerting and counting, the body can be subdued. 'Willpower' is peddled as an inexhaustible resource, and one that reflects personal worth. All that's required is perfection – accompanied by shame, and absolute repentance for the body's continual weakness and failures.

The counting and the weighing. Saying (and saying loudly) *no, no, I don't do that any more*. It's so within my control – even as it's slipping through my fingers – *I've got this*. Numbers are solid and irrefutable – so soothing, so real. The time spent concentrating, deeply, on morphing into a better version of yourself is rewarding and meaningful. Gender and sexuality philosopher Cressida J Heyes observes that 'it is a feminist commonplace that many women's achievements go unrecognized or are invisible. Losing weight, however, provokes ready congratulation; it is tangible, and can be graphed and tracked; it has setbacks and successes that seem clear-cut'.

When dieting, I become less, and the shrinking can be displayed as a downward curve on a graph. I am smaller, I am weaker, I am lighter, I am more timid. I am preoccupied, always, with the boundaries of my body – what goes in, what comes out. And I still lose. No matter how hard I try, I cannot build myself a destination. I shrink, and continue trying to shrink, and I still can't seem to disappear right. I never arrive.

My body – monstrous – returns again. The more I try

to shove it inside new packaging, the more monstrous it becomes. Uncontrollable. Out of control. (These things are the same, but different, too.) I wonder whether this focus on food – here, in this project; in life in general – is a way for me to justify my consumption, which at times has been quite incredible. Is it a way of looking back at versions of myself that have been less in control than I'd thought at the time and excusing that behaviour? A way of ridding myself of all this shame?

No matter how I try to dump my body, it just keeps coming back, because I live here.

4

The process of building a life – of becoming who you are – is a slow and continuous one. Having now entered my fourth decade, I feel like things are beginning to settle, but can't be entirely sure – either way, I now feel fiercely protective of the life I have built. I lived for this long and own what remains, for better or worse.

What remains is a life of sound – music, readings, discussion, sharing. It's a life among my people; my loyal and fiercely beloved few. It's a life where I can see the sneaker waves of my depression building, and I can sprint my hardest and still get caught out – but it's also a life where I am learning to see the signs of those waves approaching, and finding new ways to cope. I expect to always be learning this.

The cyclical flow of seasonal foods pulls me along with the passage of time. Another fucking apple, swinging chaos into the shortest and darkest day of the year, and I haven't left the house in four days, nor showered – it seems useless; the world feels like nothing but water anyway. Eventually, though, always, the arrival of nectarines and the lifting of the veil. Sticky, juicy hands; stretchy daylight; cold foods supporting happiness rather than despondency.

In my adult life, I have created new routines again and

again. New and old habits battle it out, and not everything sticks. One thing that has – even (and especially) alongside eating in complicated ways – is my newfound ability to find solace in cooking from scratch. Cooking because I elect to, for pleasure, slows food down. My connection to the outside world becomes one not of desperate consumption or using it to break my body, but one of nourishment, fun and calm.

All these things, and I among them, become elements of the natural world: animal, vegetable, mineral. The actions of connection with food eventually translate to my own presence in my body, and a renewed joy in eating.

I am learning that there is another way. A lightness.

—

In the last year or two, I have been attending a plus-sized clothing market in Melbourne. I remember my first quite clearly, because its existence filled me with hope and assurance. I left my self-disgust at the door.

There were over thirty market stalls stacked with clothing in sizes that fit me. There was also jewellery, the kind of thing I'd normally turn to at a 'straight-sized' market or clothing store, because I know that jewellery has a chance of fitting, while clothing probably won't. Or at least, my clothing choices will be few, and limited not to what I like but to the small handful of things that fit. Most mainstream retail stores go up to a size 16 if you're lucky. Mostly, I don't go clothes shopping for this reason. My wardrobe has, until recently, featured a handful of low-quality items on high rotation. These are clothes that don't make me feel good, and I wear them every day.

Generally, when clothes shopping, I approach a stand of clothing and shuffle to its far end, shame building as each clothes hanger clicks forward, checking whether an item comes in my size before allowing myself to fall in love with it. When my size isn't there – and it most often isn't – then I feel people in the store looking at me, their gaze piercing my large and irregular body. I imagine them whispering to one another about how I'm kidding myself to be shopping there in the first place. Like this body could ever carry anything flattering. As if anything could flatter this size and shape.

The plus-size market felt different. The women at this market – those both selling and buying – wore bright colours and loud prints: these clothes were the opposite of quiet, or blending in, and all those other things I routinely try to force my body into despite itself. These women looked fantastic, proud. Mostly, they seemed comfortable and at ease in their bodies.

I didn't look at sizes, trying to remember how widely they can vary between brands, particularly at the top end of size ranges. I didn't judge myself for picking up any particular size. I zeroed in on items that I thought would fit me, and I tried some on. I ended up with multiple items to choose between – I couldn't remember the last time this had happened.

'How did you go?' The woman whose stall I was trying clothes from smiled at me. These clothes used to be hers. Our bodies fit into the same clothing. We are alike.

'They both fit', I answered, startled to be in this situation. I was more used to trying things on then emerging from the change room saying, 'No luck, thanks', and leaving the clothes I liked behind, because the clothes I liked and the clothes that fit were necessarily two different things.

My body expanded with gratitude at being surrounded by so many women who looked like me, and I didn't mind taking up the space I needed.

—

There's no shortage of euphemisms: Heavy set. Big boned. Larger. Portly. Rotund. Round. Big.

There are whole generations of women who lower their voices in conspiracy and scrunch their faces when they say 'big'.

'People of size'. Aren't we all 'of size'? Some are of smaller size, others are of larger sizes. The implication of 'people of size' is that one of these things is not like the others – one of these 'sizes' is wrong.

'Plus-sized' – I don't mind that one so much. A plus, like a bonus. More than you thought you were getting, in a good way. Score.

'Fat' is most often seen as an insult, spat or whispered or anonymised. Fat activists reclaim the word 'fat'. Self-identifying as fat turns this once-hurtful word into a neutral descriptor. Using it in sentences filled with love and attaching it to kind, caring actions and stories make 'fat' a useless insult.

The past year or two has felt like a critical tipping point

for body acceptance and fat activism. I turned my attention towards this work because I had started to doubt my previous certainty about the badness of my body. I started to wonder whether food might be allowed to mean something different for me, even though I live in this body. Fat activism challenged me, and challenged my beliefs. Once the first few bricks were knocked loose, the wall of my certainty began to crumble ever more quickly.

Looking at the history of the movement, I learned that this is not the first wave of fat activism – what's currently going on is, in fact, the third wave. Like the history of many social movements, the groundwork for all of this thinking has been laid by those with the most marginal experiences – fat bodies, but in particular, black, queer, disabled bodies. The first wave of fat activism began in the United States in the late 1960s, and peaked in 1978 with the publication of Susie Orbach's seminal book *Fat Is a Feminist Issue*, which called for an end to dieting, and suggested that fat discrimination and broken relationships with food and the body are outcomes of patriarchy and oppression. Fat as rebellion, as weapon, as defence.

The second wave rolled in in the 1990s. Naomi Wolf's *The Beauty Myth* significantly shaped the thinking of a generation of women. During this time, the ideas introduced in first-wave fat activism became more widely discussed, making their way into serious research and formal programs helping those with problematic eating habits, and letting go the judgement imposed by those without such issues.

This third, more recent, wave exists in a world that looks vastly different to that of previous fat acceptance and activist battles. With the same old moralistic diet culture existing alongside a rebranded but otherwise quite similar 'wellness' culture, the current pervasiveness of image-based advertising and idealised food and body messaging is also unavoidable. While these things may be more difficult to escape, they're also fat activism's best tools. Third-wave fat activism fights for increased representation, for inclusivity, for the right to live a life free of judgement and shame, and it uses the collective power and visual force of the internet to do those things. Ideas are accessible, pushing for inter-sectionality (when they're good), and the opportunities to raise your voice are more democratic. While it's still consid-ered radical for a fat person to feel okay in their body, these ideas are gaining an increasingly wide audience. Pockets and communities exist where fat people can feel accepted, even celebrated.

You can't shame me any more, fat activism says. I will not be ashamed.

—

In the article 'Hello, I Am Fat', journalist and fat activist Lindy West addresses her boss, Dan Savage, who's well known for being sex-positive and generally quite accepting, and whose past fat-phobic comments came as something of a shock. Challenging Savage about his comments on which bodies should be allowed to wear which clothes (namely, low-slung jeans, and not-fat bodies), West 'comes out' as fat, and explains her own relationship with her body, in a blog post including a full-body photo of herself.

'I have lived in this body my whole life', she says, describing the attitude she has long held. 'I have wanted to change this body my whole life. I have never wanted anything as much as I have wanted a new body.'

Directly tackling Savage's comments, she writes:

'I get that you think you're actually helping people and society by contributing to the fucking Alp of shame that crushes every fat person every day of their lives … But you're not helping. Shame doesn't work. Diets don't work. Shame is a tool of oppression, not change.'

In a job where she could hide her body if she wished, West's 'coming out' is a bold choice. She might equally have chosen to be bodiless Lindy West, whose readers didn't even consider her appearance. By introducing herself as fat, West made herself vulnerable. She opened herself up for honest conversations but also to trolling – the kind that women receive routinely online, and the kind that is fed by admissions of having a body at all, particularly a not-male one, let alone a fat one. West's strength in this move becomes a beacon.

—

In a 2012 study, a group of European researchers found that when exposed to images of varying body types, subjects come to favour the body type they are exposed to most often.

People's pictures of themselves form in similar ways to how tastes in food are formed – or indeed, how our tastes to anything form. In the late 1960s, Robert B Zajonc coined the term 'mere exposure' while looking at the ways we come to prefer things purely because they're familiar. This is why I watch *Little Women* (the 1994 version) at least once a year – even though I know the ending: just because I know it so well; because I know the crushing pain in Beth's passing and I keep coming back anyway. The familiarity is its reward. 'Mere exposure' is the reason why people come to like the foods they grow up with – repetition leads to fondness. It's why thin bodies are desired (by ourselves, by society) – because they're the bodies we are shown. They're the bodies we know best, whether they look like our own bodies or not.

In the 2012 study, the more thin bodies test subjects were exposed to, the more they came to prefer thin bodies. In fact, when images are distorted repeatedly in similar ways (for example, a face being made to smile), an undistorted image will be seen to be doing the opposite (frowning, rather than being expressionless). These two ideas have a lot to say about how we learn what body types are acceptable, and what we perceive non-conforming bodies to be doing. I'm forced to think of all the advertising I am surrounded by that show thin people being happy, bigger people being miserable, or both. My own body is not a thin body. A thin body is good. Because mine is not a thin body, it is bad. Because mine is not a thin body it is an unhappy one, it will always be an unhappy one, and it is destined for problems – or so the logic goes.

And this isn't just adults. A different study showed that from the age of three, children are able to differentiate between body sizes, and associate negative characteristics with larger bodies.

How can we treat our bodies with kindness if we think they're unworthy of it? How can a body be repaired if it's repeatedly broken through self-hatred?

—

In her essay collection *Shrill*, West emphasises the importance of curating a media environment where you can see your own body reflected. I reached this part of the book the day after I had joined Instagram to tap into body-positive accounts that are unavailable on other platforms.

'There was really only one step to my body acceptance', she says. 'Look at pictures of fat women on the Internet until they don't make you uncomfortable any more.' She cites actor and photographer Leonard Nimoy's 'Full Body Project' (pictures of fat women being joyous, comfortable, honest and real in their bodies) as beginning her journey to self-love, followed by blogs and Instagram accounts that promote body positivity, particularly for fat women.

On the Monday morning after joining Instagram, I opened the app to be greeted by an image of a woman whose body looked like mine. I'd decided to create an account after Melbourne artist and mental health advocate Honor Eastly posted a 'belfie' (butt selfie), including a call for people to share the accounts they follow to make them feel okay about their own bodies. I investigated all the suggestions with interest, but soon realised that creating my own Instagram account was the only way I could keep all these fantastic new resources in the same place. My feed, the day after joining, was joyous: a fat woman in a swimsuit, a badge expressing the wish that I 'Have a fucking mystical day', and a poster (from @bodyposipanda) telling me, 'You're allowed to love yourself: Not when you lose 10 kilos or can fit in those jeans or get a job or a boyfriend or run 5 miles but now'. This poster quickly became my phone screensaver, and I marched into the day with the knowledge that I was backed up by strong, clever women who insist on building their own narratives. I existed in the world knowing that women like me were in love with themselves, and even if I might not encounter those women during my day, or inhabit a similarly encouraging offline world, they still existed in my safe little Instagram bubble of body positivity and acceptance.

Outside of that bubble, the world is harder. Instagram is a slow, kind social media platform. Curated in the right way, it's a soft place where I can be encouraged, nurtured and honest. Most importantly, it's a place where I see bodies that look like mine, not just as okay, and not just as tolerable: joyous. Laughing and living. Instagram is the home of the first selfie I took and didn't feel even remotely unsure about. A photo of myself that I like: a minor miracle. In the picture, taken from a high angle, I look up at the camera through my eyelashes. A soft filter makes the backlight from the window behind me an ethereal glow. I'm wearing a V-necked silk dress – emerald, with peach roses in the pattern. So often in pictures, I have trouble smiling. I become overaware of my face, and trying to arrange a smile feels strange enough to confuse my features – but in this picture, I'm just smiling. The way I would smile at someone if I were trying to make them feel welcome. Maybe it's the filter and the cleavage I was sporting that day, but it hadn't happened before.

Seeing fat bodies represented in a loving way is everything. It's getting better: in 2019, *Shrill* became a TV series on the Hulu network starring *Saturday Night Live*'s Aidy Bryant. West has repeatedly spoken of her insistence that at no point in the show would the lead character Annie step on a scale, look down and sigh. Season 1 features Annie making decisions about reproductive rights, and having sex with different people, and her family dynamics – all facets of a normal life. In 2019 also, Lizzo happened – this plus-size queen came into the mainstream consciousness and taught us all how to prioritise self-worth over external validation, how to shout compliments at ourselves the way we would to a friend, and how a large body can be a source of power. Meanwhile, in London, a Nike store displayed its fitness wear on a plus-size mannequin. These consciousness shifts aren't only happening in popular culture – in late 2018, an article called 'Everything You Know About Obesity Is Wrong' appeared on HuffPost's *Highline*. This was a humanising, comprehensive long-form piece packed with studies, statistics and irrefutable evidence for why it's time for a paradigm shift away from 'barbaric' fat shaming. The article quickly went viral.

These examples aren't the norm, or the majority, but they make it easier to curate. There are places to point now.

I try to orchestrate my own mere exposure and unlock a sense of permission. In the presence of this kind of media, I feel myself unfurling. They aren't simply pictures, but validation: your body is okay, your body is acceptable, your body is sufficient. Beyond that: your body is great. You are not too much, you are exactly enough. Your body is to be celebrated. This is radical.

—

So much is said about the 'obesity epidemic', which insists that body size is linked to health – which it's not; not that simply. The Health at Every Size (HAES) movement champions setpoint theory – the idea that a body's size is genetically predetermined, and that it will find that point naturally if only we stop interfering. Not only will the body find its comfortable setpoint, but it will fight like hell to stay there. This movement recognises that diets just don't work. When we do interfere with our body's size and shape – and we often do, through diets that pre-scribe what, when or how much to eat – the body fights back. Metabolism slows when the body panics because it can't tell the difference between a diet and starvation. Thinking about food becomes obsessional as hunger kicks into overdrive. It's basic self-preservation, honed by thousands of years of evolution. If only we could put down our weapons, and let go the restrictive or panicked rela-tionships between our bodies and the world – the ways we eat, the ways we move. HAES suggests that the body knows best, and is backed by significant evidence pointing to 'healthful behaviours' as a better indicator of health and wellbeing than body size.

The medical establishment's traditional view favours the BMI framework, which uses an individual's mass and height to derive a magic number – this is plotted on a graph alongside other magic numbers. The section of the body mass index (BMI) table deemed healthiest is termed 'normal' – with 'underweight' falling to its left, and 'overweight' and 'obese' falling to its right. Defining this 'healthy' section as 'normal' erases everything that falls outside of that zone. The unspoken word that captures everything beyond the 'normal' zone is its opposite: 'abnormal'. That word comes with connotations of dysfunction, maladjustment, a failure to toe the line. And that's just what all these other weight categories are – a failure of the body to measure up to the categories we place around it, determining who fits in the world and who doesn't.

The BMI has been criticised for lacking nuance, using height and weight as its only determinants – looking straight over age, sex, ethnicity, shape, muscle mass (which weighs more than fat), and anything else that's going on in the body. Used as the only measure of a person's wellness, BMI is a woefully inadequate authority to consult to find out whether our bodies are acceptable or not. Whether we are okay in the world. Whether this body is a body that's worthy of respect, or one to be loathed and punished.

A move from BMI to HAES frameworks shifts faith, trust and judgement from external conditions (a number, a table, a meal plan, a calorie count, a pass/fail) to the individual's own body cues, an ability to heal a potentially dysfunctional relationship with food, and move towards calmness and clarity in relation to food and the body.

'Obesity' is mid-section shots on the nightly news, where bodies move differently and uncomfortably, and don't fit into clothing; obesity is pressing flesh.

Obesity is pathologising, policing what people eat in the name of public health, assuming that a person cannot know their body well enough to provide what it needs.

Obesity is the assumption that anyone owes anyone else their health, or their body shape or size, or that any of those things are under our permanent wilful control.

Obesity is shame, and pressure, and judgement, and blame. Obesity is moral imperative.

'Obesity' is not a neutral term.

—

My usual 'No luck, thanks' change-room routine implies that luck is the main thing involved in finding clothes that fit me well. Or that I might be particularly *blessed* to find something I like. It ignores the systematic blocking-out of plus-sized clothing in 'mainstream' stores.

I hadn't realised the extent to which I had internalised this stuff, and the extent to which clothes shopping made me feel ashamed until I was in a setting where that feeling was gone. Standing in that market I realised I had permission to be comfortable in my body. I didn't feel ashamed by seeking out a clothing size that would fit me – I felt I was allowed to appraise clothes for their size and shape, and select one item that looked as if it might fit me, without looking at the label. Without worrying about how the number on that label would reflect on me, or how I might be judged by the person I was buying this clothing from. Lindy West says there was really only one step to her body acceptance. To mine, there were more, and this was perhaps number two – letting go the numbers.

A turning point. I had been unable to name the loneliness I had been feeling in my body for much of my life until I found others like me, and it was only then that I could see the aloneness for what it was. I didn't realise that I didn't see myself reflected in any of the media or culture I was consuming, until I found my own body looking back at me from my carefully curated Instagram feed. I didn't realise I'd thought fat bodies had to be sad until I saw fat bodies being radiant and joyous.

Eventually, the force of evidence saying that 'fat' might not be what I'd always believed became irrefutable. It was with quite some shock and discomfort that I learned there's nothing *wrong* with my body; the world just isn't made for me. Or for people who live in bodies like mine. And that's not okay.

5

The thing that has always held my family together most strongly is food. I wonder if this is the case for all families. Perhaps it's a timeless image – a family gathered around a table with food at its centre. Over a breakfast bar, or a sink. Seated together on a picnic rug, reaching across a boat, looking down at a freshly felled animal. Humans come together, again and again, over food.

Or perhaps the attraction is that food is possibly the best and only proper way to show you care, on a level so elemental: by saying 'I'll help you live'. I'll nourish your body, so you can continue to *be*. Your existence matters to me, so let me help it.

Perhaps food is the thing that keeps all families connected. Perhaps it has to be.

Dad and I bond over what, how and why we've been eating – an echo of when I was young and he would let me find recipes we could make together, or gave me something new to try for the first time. I would flick through the *Women's Weekly* cookbooks on the shelves that lined the study, appraising the glistening piles of food pictured, or look at the black-and-white low-resolution images in Dad's Dutch culinary school textbook – it only happened occasionally, when he had (rare) time off work, but those days when we cooked together were such an intimate treat. This was how he passed down the values he had accumulated over his years working in kitchens – his was a very specific parenting expertise:

Taste everything.

What's said in the kitchen stays in the kitchen.

Work. Work really hard.

This advice has so often helped. The precious moments Dad and I spent together in kitchens and around food blaze in my memory, and we attempt to recreate them now, shuffling close to the fire at the heart of our relationship.

Mum and I have spent much of our lives talking together about what we're not eating. She has been dieting for as long as I can remember. We have spent long conversations comparing our efforts at suppression, at prodding our overweight bodies into more acceptable shapes. Swapping numbers. Together, we'd try to get it right; striving to correct ourselves. Often, Mum and I would swap recipes and ask about weight loss, and then say nothing when we inevitably failed to change our habits. These habits asserted themselves as stubborn and unchangeable, but we found some comfort in our shared battle.

Mum lives with schizoaffective disorder, and this means that when she's unwell she becomes manic, obsessing and diving too deeply into projects. At the extremes of this condition, she becomes unreachable. On a day-to-day level, though, it's just a part of her life.

When Mum is thrown into disarray and confusion, she loses herself in time and place, believing she's elsewhere, or else-*when*. During a psychotic episode, she hears voices and senses messages in everything – her world becomes semiotically overwhelming. When she's beyond any care that can be given at home, she spends time in hospital. This happened occasionally when I was too young to remember, before the respite of an uneventful decade. But after that quiet patch, during which I did much of my growing up, psychotic episodes came once a year, then twice a year, then every couple of months for one whole year. When I was a child, Dad often sheltered me from Mum's most unwell moments, and I only knew what I absolutely needed to – *Mum's getting better in hospital*, or *Mum's spending some time with Oma and Opa*. He managed to downplay or make me laugh about the absurd aspects of those situations, and with Dad in charge it felt manageable. As an adult, I am far more aware of my own role in Mum's care. I sense when her illness approaches and makes itself known, like a drum beating in the distance, then growing louder and clearer before thundering to crescendo.

At points during my adolescence I came home to a pile of tupperware containers stacked on top of the microwave, which meant Mum had been baking. And not just the odd batch of biscuits, but as if she was playing a game she intended to win, baking four different cakes, biscuits or slices all at once. What might otherwise look like a productive day raised red flags in our house – this was Mum in overdrive. We were being cared for, but care combined with mania can be smothering. That's not to say she became incapable when unwell – at a certain point, she became *over*-capable (the baked goods, or the furniture in the lounge moved around, or the plastics cupboard newly, beautifully organised). While she looked for messages in any available medium (television, radio, newspapers, books, sheet music, bibles, films), it was the sudden, dramatic increase in capability that told us she was in decline.

This mania has manifested in the other direction, too, turning Mum's enthusiasm for doing good inwards, against her, against her body.

Mum's weight fluctuations – much like my own – seem connected with her mental health. It's not a direct correlation. But Mum's mental health also isn't *un*important in its impact on how she lives in her body. I don't want to set Mum apart because of this, and I don't want it to discount other parts of this story. The causes are multiple and none of them stand alone. This rat-king of worries and hopes, tails all tied together, fighting for space and directional pull.

Mum's mental health is often a consideration, in all things (in this thing? Yes, in this thing too), and this means we lean away from difficult topics when we talk. 'What's for dinner?' is a safe question to ask; it can't drag in trauma or confusion – and besides, food is nourishment, right? To eat well is to be well. Striking a balance between appetite and control is a marker of health – apart from when it's not. All that aside, like so many other kids with their mothers, I have watched Mum diet on and off since I was young. Food, here, has become cause for suspicion.

I grew up with both my parents' attitudes inside me: I love food and I hate it. It nurtures me and it is dangerous. I feel the pull between these two influences. To begin unpicking the knot, I have questioned and questioned and questioned.

What does food mean to me?

How and why does this matter?

If my parents sit at opposing ends of a spectrum, where do I fall along that line?

Is it a line? Do I fall at all?

I yearn for the two opposing halves to make a whole, or at the very least for this see-saw to quit its totter and sit balanced and safe. I want to not negotiate every time I eat.

And yet I also wonder if this is just the order of things – if, as the child of these two particular people, this is what my attitudes have to be. I wonder whether, for my brother (who also became a chef), these halves exist at all. As a man living in a less politicised body, perhaps this isn't a factor for him.

It's nobody's responsibility. It just, so curiously, is. It's difficult not to see memoir as a kind of calling-to-account, or assignment of blame. An exercise in checks and balances, or a tally. I'd rather think of it as questioning and seeking. I'm chasing my memories down, following them around. Trailing torn-up fragments of self with a sense of hope, as desperate as that hope may be.

The stories my family tell are often food stories. These stories are warmth and home; reliable and exciting at once. In a way, we have agreed that to feed is to care. To eat is to build upon our collective story. I remember. *We* remember. We use food to say, again and again, who we are.

—

The internet is littered with pictures of meals; diners go out in search of increasingly elaborate or novel dishes (and I don't just mean theatrical – the humblest dishes can be novel, too – witness gastropubs' adoption of gourmet cheese toasties or luxury mac and cheese); and we're becoming more skilled at preparing impressive food at home. Proficiency with food has become a form of social capital. Cooking as a hobby is deeply concerned with aesthetics, and many home cooks are now able to make their food look (and taste) like restaurant quality. We have access to so much, and to such high-quality foodstuffs, but we've also come to expect and demand these things, taking them for granted. In the course of any given day we prepare beautiful food, create images of the beautiful food that's prepared for us by others, and then we go home and watch beautiful people creating more beautiful food on TV. During ad breaks (selling food or ways to avoid food), we consult online streams displaying what our friends are eating. *Food and screens, food and screens.* We buy books that show us how to make beautiful food. During my time as a bookseller, customers would often admit to me that they'd amassed a mountain of gorgeous cookbooks, but only ever looked at the pictures. Eating with our eyes and minds can sometimes be enough. More than ever before, we're daring to try – and performing our daring as we try – new and strange foods. What we eat, where, how, and with whom have become powerful methods of building social and cultural capital. The ability to access the 'right', Instagrammable meals is a class marker in itself.

We feed on the feeds, snapping and posting our food

to display as part of our social media consumption. *(To say, again and again, who we are.)* But I think there's also something deeply interesting and essential about knowing what your friends are eating. While 'pictures of people's breakfast' is an easy criticism to level at 'self-obsessed' social media users, it discounts how fun and compelling it is to see what's going into your friends' mouths, and how enjoyable it is to compare. The best breakfast pictures show us what people feed each other: a birthday brunch, or friends nursing one another through recovery (whether from a night of merriment, or serious illness).

So often, the information that comes through those feeds leans towards the notion of responsibility and wholesomeness. This hangs over the relationship people have to their food, meaning that what we choose to consume becomes loaded with political and ethical considerations, on top of the performative aspects of consumption. We are encouraged to question whether we are treating our bodies, our planet, and each other well. This domain of 'things eaten', once so private and personal, is now open to public censure. What to eat is morally loaded. Maybe it always has been so, but now it feels different – there seems to be some new element at play: performativity.

The timbre of the discussion around food has changed – it's become more frantic. The rising sense of panic is based in bleak and worrying fact. On the problem of food waste alone, there's this shocking statistic: up to a third of Australian-grown produce never makes it to supermarkets because of the unreasonable cosmetic standards that demand a perfectly bent banana, a shiny apple, a straight carrot. One in five bags of food purchased as household groceries gets thrown out: the waste tally grows and grows. Food production globally – most of it on the large-scale, high-yield, industrial model – accounts for about a third of greenhouse gas emissions. These are just a handful of examples.

The urgency of our ecological peril, the extreme dysfunction of food production systems, and the confusion many people feel about how to eat well – it's all hitting fever pitch.

There's a sense that food is also, somehow, an expression of our selves – an extension and performance of who we *are*. The fuel aspect of food has been perfected, and it now dovetails neatly with 'clean eating' and 'health' discourse – we're fluent in the meaning and benefits of macro and micronutrients: food science has sculpted our needs into a to-do list of vitamins, minerals, preventative measures and nutritional efficiency, and for the most part we know just how to tick things off the list in the course of any given day. What we're less familiar with is everything that simmers beneath the 'food-is-simple' science. We're less good at unpacking what food really *means* to us beyond the extraction of energy, and making space for those stories.

I feel a pang of hot embarrassment when a *MasterChef* contestant fails to replicate a dish that demonstrates their heritage. The pride these contestants have in where they come from is suddenly dashed – the custard splits, the sauce burns, the skin doesn't crisp as it should. These cooks have failed to share what they love, the things that mean love to them – their synonyms for love, their whispers of home.

And they're not just letting themselves down, but letting down everything that rode on that dish. Sorry Mum, sorry Dad, sorry grandparents. Sorry, family history. Sorry heritage, and the riptide of time. Sorry, whole massive weight of country of origin. Sorry childhood, sorry family dining table. Sorry; so sorry. They've failed in asserting who they are through their food.

—

I have returned to food again and again in my writing. The first piece I wrote on food and family was about my brother, Chris.

'I'd like to write about your kitchen', I told him. 'For uni. I'd like to sit and watch you during service for a night or two, and just take notes.'

At the time, he worked in the kitchen of a pub close to the Victorian border. It had a wine bar on site, and the menu spanned pub classics, kids' meals, woodfired pizzas, and the more creative specials (duck ravioli, lamb slow roast).

'Why?' he laughed.

It was hard to answer. One reason was that I simply felt I didn't have access to any other experiences that would satisfy the expectations of the immersion journalism assignment, and I'd always been fascinated by the heat and action of kitchens. I was drawn to the mystery and the drive. But there was more to it, of course.

He seemed a bit baffled, but agreed. If nothing else, we'd get a nice weekend in a shared space – something we too often miss out on.

'We can't talk though', I explained. 'It's a fly-on-the-wall thing. So I'll watch, you do whatever you normally do. I'll take notes until I've seen enough, and then I'll leave.'

On the first night, I brought a notebook and pen from my upstairs bedroom down to the pub kitchen. I lay my notebook out on the chest freezer – my desk for the evening – and teetered on the bar stool I'd been given. Soon Chris sidled up to me with a 'spare' pot of cider in his burnt and calloused hand. He put it casually on top of the freezer and returned to the stove. Running out of bench space for 'spare' chips, he soon furnished me with a full meal of 'spares'. I ate; I jotted. We didn't talk, but he couldn't bear to know I was there and not feed me.

It was strange to be so close to him again. Chris first left home when he was still quite young – adolescence was difficult for him, and he spent it breaking just about every rule he could find. He left before I was a teenager myself, so sometimes our adulthood has been our opportunity to catch up on that close time that siblings normally get (fighting, lounging) together. Watching him from the corner of his kitchen, I saw both a stranger and someone I knew intimately. For the most part, we don't talk very much. We send each other pictures of our dinner from time to time, or compare notes via text message about how busy we are. The meals we share together in an average year could be counted on one hand.

My food writing continued after this – I wrote about my Dad's advice that *What's said in the kitchen stays in the kitchen*, and how it provides a good template for resilience in the world outside of kitchens, too. I wrote about Dutch food for a collection of first- and second-generation migrants' food stories. I branched outside my family and wrote about food films and the cultural significance of dietary choice.

It's magnetic, and I have kept coming back to food, trying to pin the mystical to the page. The magic and fear that I find in equal measure in food keeps drawing me back in.

—

Food forms a chain around my family and me: connecting, binding and tethering. My memories link, one to another, connecting where I hadn't realised they might or should. But memory is like that, isn't it? Entwined; even circular. Everything we know is in there, and everything comes back eventually, bound to something – everything – else.

'I'm eating rainbow popcorn; I'm in the pool; I'm in Lake Eildon; I'm holding Dad's shoulders' – other people share their food memories with me, and I'm surprised to see that the freefalling is common. Memory is a strange place, with steps and ladders, and sinkholes. Memory slips from one time and place into another. A food and a story go hand in hand. A moment and a flavour. When we eat, those memories rush back, because our bodies harbour so much without our even knowing it.

As my relationship with my body and with food has changed, I've found myself trying to unpack the questions that mystify me: why are we so very tangled up over something that's just meant to fuel the body? Isn't it simple? Aren't we over-complicating this?

Nobody exists in a vacuum, and food culture is human culture. There is no opting out.

In 1825, French gourmand Jean Anthelme Brillat-Savarin wrote: 'Animals feed themselves; men eat; but only wise men know the art of eating'. Food is not just necessity, but can aspire to be art. This was in his cornerstone text *The Physiology of Taste*. In it, he takes an approach typical of the era, setting out rules, priorities and observations about what and how Parisians at the time 'should' have been eating. It's an instruction manual of sorts, including dedications to and arguments with his friends – transcriptions of the kinds of talk that goes on over a meal. It was published nearly 200 years ago, but much of it is recognisable, and still applies in today's culinary landscape. In an early dialogue, Brillat-Savarin portrays a friend as telling him, 'The single word *gastronomy* makes everyone prick up his ears. The subject is always fashionable. And mockers like to eat, as well as the rest'. Haters gonna eat.

The subject is always fashionable: more recently, Heston Blumenthal has become the poster boy for this kind of over-complication of mealtime. He crafts gelatinous spheres of flavour, foams and ice creams that taste of freshly cut grass, wet soil, bacon and eggs, or childhood in the 1970s. He uses theatrical trickery to delight and bemuse. He draws diners' bodies *and* minds to the table for an 'immersive experience'. Heston's whole point is complication, and a generation of cooks have followed suit. The *MasterChef* kitchen all too often looks more like a science lab. Mastery of food, in this way, stands in for some other kind of power – access to knowledge, skills, status and often a masculine proficiency with gadgetry. Our modern gastronomical gurus still aspire to art within their cookery.

I'm not interested in food that looks like something else. There's so much fuss around theatrical food, but I'm not interested in food that trundles out on a bed of chemical smoke. I'm not interested in superfoods that will increase my life expectancy or sex drive or make me glow hot pink. I'm not interested in foods that act – by appearance, by flavour – like something they're not. I'm just not all that interested in food that feels dishonest.

Because I've written about food, I sometimes get labelled a 'food writer', and discussions of food writing so often arrive at the question, 'What's the strangest thing you've eaten?'

I've spoken with people who have eaten rats, or been brand ambassadors for crickets as a sustainable food source. Who've known exactly how many people can be fed from one well-butchered emperor penguin.

It's tempting to feel like a foodie failure in the face of these experiences – how can I write food well when I haven't tried the well and *truly* wacky meals?

But I'm less interested in the extraordinary foods than I am in the extraordinary effects of mundane foods.

I appreciate clever food, I enjoy occasionally novel food, but what about everything that happens in between? I don't pour nitrogen on my muesli in the mornings. What about the things that I experience every day, rather than once a year or once in a lifetime? Why do my knees go weak at the smell of leeks in butter? What have we chosen to eat? What do we eat as part of our everyday lives? What have we been surrounded by and consumed just because?

Sure, of course I'm curious about what has been the best meal and the worst – the backstreet you wandered into late at night in a foreign country, or the thing you paid a week's wages for, or the awful table you felt you couldn't leave for politeness – but feel more curiosity about the foods people eat and hardly consider. What do you do every day? And how do you relate to that? How can you feed yourself, several times each day, every day of your life, and not give that any significant thought?

How can we think about it both more, and less? How can we be more mindful, less thoughtless?

How can we be good to ourselves, our bodies, one another?

—

My family focuses on the tasty things – and there have been so many tasty things.

The squiggly chocolate shapes Dad pipes for our birthday cakes, and balances on piped domes of cream.

The slow tour Mum and I make of the cheese desk at a gallery, trying all of them before we decide which is best. Probably trying them again to make sure we agree on our evening snack.

The southern American barbecue that my brother and I pile on to our plates, groaning over the heat, the smoke, the stodgy solid comfort of it all.

We eat as entertainment. Cooking and feeding are acts of nourishment, nurturing, and care.

But there's an underside to all this that we turn our faces away from: What of hunger? What of fullness? What of craving, and bingeing, and refusal?

My parents divorced almost fifteen years ago. Mum moved out, and I lived with Dad during my final years at home, before moving to the city. Dad remarried, Mum moved on. Our family is now scattered across the country – Victoria, Western Australia, Tasmania; country, suburbs, city. There's a strait between us now, but food is still the chain that binds us.

Food is also a battleground. It's a place where I can be fiercely myself, by eating differently from my family. I rebel by eating, by not eating, by eating in ways they don't know about – ways new, foreign, or novel. Dangerous or excessive. Sometimes hidden, sometimes loud.

All I know with any certainty is that I can't remember food without thinking of my family. I can't remember my family without thinking of food.

6

My first food memory is of strawberry cream chocolates. In fact, this is my first memory of anything at all.

Memory can serve as a kind of tally – a scorecard adding up the points, assuring us of who we are. We know our own identities, and feel certain of them because memory stacks up in corroboration. Imbued with great importance, our first memory is the prime mover.

My family lived out of town. The floor of that house was made of cork. It was my third Easter, but the first where I was aware that it was a special occasion.

I remember standing in the hall near the kitchen, the cork cool under my feet. I wore a thin nightgown, and the cat pawed at my bare ankles. In my hands I held the chocolates, which came from my brother. They were arranged in a heart-shaped box, and were individually wrapped in bright pink foil. I felt precious and loved.

There are some stories my family tell again and again – like any family, we have stories we recognise from their very first words. There's a Dutch word, *gezellig*, which English fails to translate. *Gezellig* sits somewhere between cosy and comfortable, and it's related to keeping warm, friendly company. My family's stories are *gezellig* – they are about where we have come from and where we are going. They are the mythology that we balance upon – and like all myths, they exist to explain how the world works. The immovable order of things.

There's an unspoken contract within my family about which stories are to be uttered, and which we don't mention, ever. The minute someone gets uncomfortable, we stop talking. We are what we repeatedly do, and as an adult, I lean towards silence when things hurt or confuse me.

Instead, we focus on the tasty things. Discomfort is bitter and difficult to swallow. So we don't: we spit it out. It doesn't make the menu.

The French Renaissance essayist Michel de Montaigne said, 'My conscience does not falsify one tittle; what my ignorance may do, I cannot say'. North American essayist David Lazar says of the whole question of truth, 'It maketh me nervous'. Me too. I've asked about the strawberry creams, to be safe, but nobody else in the family remembers them. Does that make this an unsafe story? It doesn't feel unsafe, it feels *gezellig*.

I took the foil off the chocolate as carefully as my three-year-old motor skills allowed, leaving only small tears in it. Looking back now, I wonder how reliable my memory is. There's a possibility that I actually butchered the neat, perfect foil wrappers in my eagerness to get at the chocolate inside.

The small size of the chocolates from my brother made them more special. I remember holding the box and their smell, but not the moment when the chocolates were gone. I mean, of course – why would I? Such a moment must have come. As soon as I put a sweet, all-mine chocolate into my mouth I began to lose that gift from my brother. I guess this is what they mean when they say that you can't have your cake and eat it too. I was left only with the reflex that kicks at my memory when I smell strawberry flavouring; my careful selection of the strawberry chocolate from a Snack block or chocolate box; and the fondness I still have for smoothing out chocolate foils.

That fascinates me – the knock-on effect of one memory to another. I once read about a study where researchers used mice in a maze to explore the idea of 'associated memories'. Playing a tone to the mice before administering an electric shock, the researchers found that the mice learned to associate the two. The mice froze in fear on hearing the tone, anticipating the electric shock that would surely follow. Next, the researchers played the tone again, and administered an amnesia-inducing drug at the moment the mice remembered the shock. The next time the tone was played, the mice were unfazed. Removing the last memory of the electric shock removed *all* memories of the shock. Subsequent and follow-up research has confirmed this finding in more nuanced ways. What this provides for memory theory is some proof that when we remember something, we're actually remembering the last time we recalled that thing. This is how memories morph over time, through an elaborate game of whispers that we speak to ourselves.

Neuroscientist Yadin Dudai suggests that keeping original memories intact is close to impossible. 'If you have a memory', he says, 'the more you use it, the more you are likely to change it … The safest memories are the memories which are in the brain of people who cannot remember' – but I *can* remember, and I've been thinking on this strawberry creams memory all my life. Every other memory I have spins forth from this one.

These chocolates are the first present I remember receiving; the first thing I'm conscious of owning all for myself – a gift of food from my brother. We repeat this action again and again, he and I, until our adult relationship is almost entirely based around giving and receiving food, tasting and critiquing, trying novel things. He wants me to taste his duck ravioli; to tell him I enjoy it; to acknowledge that he has made this for me. I watch as he fusses the rocket around my plate and positions the pasta with sculptural flourish. I know that he's been more particular with my plate than he has with the others. I am cared for.

If I were to visit my three-year-old self and remove that strawberry cream chocolate, what about my life might be different? Would I still know, unshakably, that my brother loves me? Would we both still be giving each other food gifts all these years later?

Considering her own first memory, Virginia Woolf said that 'if life has a base that it stands upon, if it is a bowl that one fills and fills and fills – then my bowl without a doubt stands upon this memory'. I imagine my life as a marble bowl, hefty and wide, which teeters on a tiny, pink foil-wrapped chocolate.

7

Where you come from is inherited because it is fed to you. What's inside you becomes what's inside you.

On the Greek island of Kalymnos, food, family and memory are tied inextricably together. Common parlance urges residents and visitors to 'eat, in order to remember Kalymnos'. Food is something for Kalymnian families to gather around – as it is for so many families all over the world – but it's also the centrepiece of religious and social rituals, and this gives food a weighty significance.

Food-giving acts symbolically for Kalymnians, who see the exchange of food gifts as a way to build community and honour the food gifts given – and received – by their ancestors throughout history. The Kalymnian memory for food is long; intergenerational. Food gifts must be accepted, and when the gift is eaten, debt (between the giver and the recipient) is internalised. 'I owe you' sits in the belly. I wonder whether the Kalymnians feel weighed down or comfortably anchored.

But then I know what this feels like, really. It feels like setting the agenda – not in a cynical or calculated way. It's establishing a safety net. It feels like stating, 'I owe you', on the most basic level, because a family is primarily a survival unit – it provides and shares food and shelter.

In his long essay *Salad Days*, writer and editor Ronnie Scott looks at the ways people use food to communicate, and what kinds of messages they send through their food consumption choices. After eating a once-in-a-lifetime, $500 meal at Danish gastronomical destination Noma, Scott wonders whether he can justify this kind of spending on food, and what the ethical implications are of spending his limited income in this way. Placing his own story among broader social concerns, he wonders why the young middle class are so willing to spend comparatively large amounts of money on expensive fare (or, as current media scares would have baby boomers believe, moderately expensive fare, like the much-maligned $20 avocado toast brunch) rather than investing in housing or other more enduring purchases. One of the reasons Scott suggests for this behaviour is that 'our engagements with food can be powerfully expressive of other things we love and want'. In this, he echoes prominent food writer MFK Fisher's musing in the preface to her food memoir *The Gastronomical Me*, where she says:

> It seems to me that our three basic needs, for food and security and love, are so mixed and mingled and entwined that we cannot straightly think of one without the others. So it happens that when I write of hunger, I am really writing about love and the hunger for it, and warmth and the love of it and the hunger for it.

The poet, academic and writer Antjie Krog claims that, 'the action of eating, of taking in food is simply enchanting – because it's the way we can take up the world inside ourselves, how what is around us becomes part of us. We eat the world'.

So consider me enchanted.

Inside our bellies, we're full of fun and enchantment, and we're full of other people's expressions of caring and nurturing. Food struggles to be just one thing, least of all a simple 'fuel'. No wonder the 'war on obesity' is producing scores of disordered eaters. No wonder so many feel broken by the encouragement to ignore their bodies and deny its basic desires. In writing, as in lived experience, these associations and this significance make food difficult. In short: it means too much. No wonder MFK Fisher couldn't think of it 'straightly'.

For Fisher, food was a vehicle for metaphor – a mode of storytelling. For her, and for Scott too, food was so much more than just fuel for the body. It's also a statement about our terms of engaging with the world, and a method of emotional expression. Food is what we pile our stories on to.

Food is one way that we learn our own origin stories – it's definitely how I learned mine.

—

Mum and Dad are both Dutch. Mum migrated to Australia when she was two, and Dad when he was seventeen. They returned to Holland after marrying, and that's where my brother was born. They came back to Tasmania before I was born, to be closer to the support of Mum's family. Both of my parents act out their heritage through the foods they enjoy, and which appeared on their own childhood tables.

A large part of my understanding of what it means to be Dutch comes from the foods I have eaten with my family.

In an essay on inheriting and performing culture in new places, writer Durga Chew-Bose says:

> What tethers me to my parents is the unspoken dialogue
> we share about how much of my character is built on
> the connection I feel to the world they were raised in but
> that I've only experienced through photos, visits, food.
> It's not mine and yet, *I get it*. First-generation kids, I've
> always thought, are the personification of déjà vu.

The foods I recognise as Dutch form a huge portion of what I know about what it means to be Dutch. I only visited Holland recently – well and truly an adult; fully cooked, so to speak – but in the Netherlands I definitely felt that déjà vu. My Dutch-ness is learned from my family, and most of what I know of being Dutch is related to specific imported food brands or my family's own interpretation of traditional dishes.

One dish that appeared on our table regularly from Mum's repertoire was braised cabbage, a rare purple food with a vinegar kick. Walking through the 'International Foods' section at Woolworths now, I find this dish in a jar. How can all those meals, all those memories, my fascination at purple food and its unique tang be squeezed into that little container? What happens when you open it? Surely it can't just be cabbage that comes out of that jar.

Also in the International Foods section are almond fingers and the chocolate-dipped biscuits whose name translates to 'goats' feet'. I used to picture Holland's fields filled with baby goats traipsing through chocolate puddles. My spirit secretly swells when I see buckets of apple syrup and boxes of chocolate sprinkles. These packets hold my memories of home.

Without these foods, my connection to what it means to be Dutch seems tenuous, at best. I was born in Australia, and have only recently been to Holland. I understand only some of the language, and speak even less. My pronunciation is poor. I cannot conjugate verbs.

—

In Australia, multiculturalism is often most acceptably expressed through foods. In primary school classrooms, I remember being given red bean paste buns in Japanese lessons, gelati in Italian lessons, and feta in religious education, to show what the shepherds would have eaten. Food builds a bridge into unfamiliar cultures. We proudly hold 'multicultural' events which mainly feature food stalls. Perhaps some dancing. Nothing threatening, like spirituality or language.

Lebanese–Australian anthropology academic Ghassan Hage calls the Australian embrace of cultural and ethnic diversity through foods a 'multiculturalism without migrants'. Rather than actual acceptance of diverse cultures, the contemporary interest in foods from other cultures represents an erasure of the lived experiences of the people who make that food in favour of a smorgasbord of choice within a capitalist, (mainly) Anglo social sphere where diners are just trying to call attention to how adventurous and worldly they are. There's economic and cultural capital tied up in this.

I benefit from existing in a time where my family's food isn't regarded with suspicion but curiosity, and in a time where sharing that food within my family is an acceptable way of feeling at home. I benefit from a heritage that isn't exoticised or forced to perform for others in order to earn its place, and this makes me lucky.

—

One particular Dutch dish has accumulated meaning for me – *patatje flip*. I can't even pronounce these words very well. Every time I try, the vowels slip around in my mouth and come out mangled. The memory of patatje flip lives in the failure of my speech, and in the taste I have for something that isn't actually a real dish.

'Patatje flip.'

Patatje flip – the proper patatje flip, as eaten in Holland – is potato fries with thick mayonnaise and satay sauce. Imperialism created a melting pot food culture in Holland, with a particularly strong Indonesian influence. This is how we arrive at satay sauce on chips.

In the past, Dad has often come up with new variations on sauce combinations, which never quite resulted in what he was searching for. I've heard it said that the last place you should look for assimilation is in a migrant's pantry – they'll hold on to their homeland's foods long after the rest of their life has blended into their new home's culture.

Although Dad now says that he's been Australian for longer than he's been Dutch, he still needs to buy the good mayo. He still makes fresh white bread sandwiches with impossibly sweet fillings. His pantry has not quite assimilated just yet.

Dad's sauce-mixing experiments fascinated and entertained me, and I felt a kind of kinship in our search for The Sauce.

But how could I participate in this search fully, when I'd never tasted the original? I didn't contribute; we were not equals in this quest. I just bore witness.

For thirty years I watched Dad attempt to recreate patatje flip sauces at the dinner table. A Dutch table – or perhaps maybe just *our* Dutch table – features condiments proudly in the middle, and whatever else might appear, mayonnaise is never missed. Not the sweet, runny commercial mayonnaise Australians favour, but thick, whole-egg mayo. The kind that forms peaks on the plate and dries clear if left on un-rinsed dishes overnight.

Jimmy's Saté Sauce is an Asian, fish-based peanut satay sauce. The closest Dad got to his real patatje flip was to combine Jimmy's Saté Sauce with whole-egg mayonnaise. The two sauces would sit side by side, with a little ooze section in the middle where the two touched. The mixing was done by chip, picking up a little of both sauces from the swirl of satay and mayo.

The burger chain Lord of the Fries was a revelation. Their hot chips are just hot chips, and nothing particularly special, but their sauce selections are the stuff of magic. I took Dad and introduced him to the Asian fries, which combine 'Belgian mayo' with satay sauce. *This is it, by another name!* I thought.

Dad chewed and tilted his head from side to side for a while.

'They're nice.'

'Are they *it*?' I asked with a smile in my voice, because I was so sure that I'd given my father a connection with his homeland – so sure that I'd found the end-point to all the sauce-mixing and searching.

'Nup.'

Even if I did find the right sauces for patatje flip, maybe this isn't what Dad's looking for.

———

There are two possible readings of Australia's enthusiasm for culturally diverse foods.

The first is that we flatten cultures down to their foods because to look deeper is scary. A one-dimensional Other is easier to make room for. It's less Other. To look deeper than another culture's food introduces truly unfamiliar things – things that we, as Australians, are likely to reject because they look too different to our own lives. At least the food is tasty.

The other explanation is that food is universal. Even in cultures that don't look or sound like our own, people have to eat. We pride ourselves on being adventurous eaters, and whether we recognise it or not, eating another culture's food is perhaps the most elemental way to let that culture in. 'The way to a man's heart is through his stomach', after all, so perhaps we're all bound by hearts and stomachs. Perhaps, while we don't quite know how to welcome people different to ourselves, it's the best we can do to share some food – the most basic of requirements, and something we definitely have in common.

The flip side of this is the symbolic rejection of other cultures' foods. Sometimes it's through ignorance – a lack of adventurousness could lead to this kind of rejection. At other times, it's a knowing act. Take Pauline Hanson's mortal fear of the halal snack pack, for example. She seems to believe it's a slippery slope – I imagine that she thinks, *If we let the snack pack into our lives, where will it all end?* There's probably something more cognisant in her thought process, too. As the owner of a fish 'n' chip shop, that beacon of childhood summers and lazy hot days, she has to know how closely people hold their food ways, even (especially) the culturally specific ways hot potato chips are eaten.

In a move that looks an awful lot like nationalism, Australian identity is reinforced by the consumption of lamb: year after year, ads from Meat and Livestock Australia home in on Australia Day, cashing in on ideas about multiculturalism and inclusiveness by giving us taglines to grab hold of. As Australia as a whole becomes more polarised in its attitudes toward multiculturalism, lamb is still suggested as the thing that brings us all together. Because 'we love our lamb'. Aside from mateship and a fair go, our love of lamb is one of the closest things we have to 'Aussie values' – our love of lamb seems less curated than those other things we hold up as symbols of Australianism. The love of lamb is a relatively recent development: pre-colonisation,

Indigenous people enjoyed tubers and wild rice, which were all but wiped out when colonisers' precious lamb trampled the carefully tended soil. As Bruce Pascoe persuasively argues in *Dark Emu*, white insistence on introduced species as the first cultivated food sources (ignoring evidence of Indigenous crops, irrigation, seed trading and surplus food storage) helped the Europeans who were stealing this land to justify their actions. Then, as now, the 'love of lamb' was raised as emblematic, triumphant.

And since a national dish is enough to define 'us', it must be enough to define anyone else, too.

—

I can point to a number of Dutch foods as evidence of my heritage. The only member of my family born in Australia, I have still inherited some approximation of my father's foreign palate.

Mayonnaise belongs on steak, chicken, fish … all protein, really. And on chips, steamed vegetables, or salads. And on anything that doesn't have a strong flavour of its own. And some things that do. My brother went through a thing with Mint Slice biscuits and mayonnaise.

Coffee shop chain Gloria Jean's recently introduced their 'coffee topper', which is not a 'coffee topper' but a Dutch *stroopwafel*.

I am most Dutch when eating, and this proved true during my visit to Holland. It was a short stay – just eight days – but I played familiar food bingo, trying as many things I recognised as possible, and comparing what I knew with what I didn't. I put my idea of Dutch food up against the actuality of Dutch food. My family introduced me to foods I'd never heard of, like the enormous *bossebol* cream-filled pastry that my uncle brought back to his apartment for morning tea.

It's said that eating is a way that we bring the outside world inside of us, assimilating it with our own bodies. Before visiting Holland I *was* the outside world. I stood outside of the world of my family, off to the side of understanding. While there I ate and ate: now that I was inside this world I'd put as much of it inside me as possible.

Of course, I'm still outside. Visiting a place for a week doesn't allow for any *real* understanding, and this is no exception. But for just a moment, I *felt* like I'd arrived home. The familiar accents were everywhere; a whole country of friendly people speaking the language of my family. The things my family had cooked for me, or brought home, or insisted wasn't quite the real thing. All in one place.

—

Dad's attempts at recreating patatje flip weren't his only Dutch food experiments. He also bought a heap of large sandwich presses (large enough to toast four sandwiches at a time if he'd wanted), and created stroopwafels that tasted far more strongly of cinnamon than the packet ones, and lacked the distinctive waffle print I recognise from the packaged biscuits. But I love all the versions of stroopwafel I've tasted: the packet versions, which Dad says aren't fresh. Dad's fresh ones, which were like another food entirely –

more cinnamon, more spice. Then there were the fresh, oozing, warm sandwiches I had made in front of me at Albert Cuyptmarkt in Amsterdam, after I managed to stammer *Een stroopwafel, alsjeblieft*. When the vendor handed me the sweet, gooey waffle he smiled and said in English, 'Hold it flat'. This was something else again.

Or another day during that visit, at another market, this time with Dad. A woman stands behind a waffle press, and we watch the dough puff and deflate. She cuts it open and smears hot syrup on using something like an icing spatula. As we stood in the sun, I handed my phone to my step-mum.

'Take a photo of us?'

Dad was visibly downcast, but he smiled for the photo.

'These *aren't the same*', he said. It was as if Holland had changed, he had changed, and now even the stroopwafels had changed, making the food of his memory a floating signifier, and the satisfaction of his cravings an impossibility.

I haven't tasted the original versions of much of the Dutch food I know and love. My palate is full of weird impostors; even if you gave me real patatje flip, I probably wouldn't enjoy it. I'd rather Jimmy and mayo.

Then there's the food that I don't know the origin of. There are some confirmed strange foods – salty, fatty herring; *hagelslag*, which describes both the chocolate sprinkles eaten on toast for breakfast and the bright white and blue or pink sugar and aniseed balls served on rusks to celebrate the arrival of a newborn. But there are also foods that could be blamed on my father's weird, nation-less palate. Those fresh strawberries on sandwiches – and it must be very, very fresh bread. That leftover rice micro-waved with brown sugar and butter to make a pudding. Lashings of butter and a thick layer of brown sugar on sandwiches after lunch, like a dessert sandwich.

Are these Dutch foods? Are these foods *anywhere*?

Chips with Jimmy paste and whole-egg mayo is not patatje flip. But it is *my* patatje flip, and it is the thing I picture when those words are spoken.

All those years that Dad spent mixing and approximating flavours have shaped my own palate for Dutch foods, and maybe they've shaped his, too. The approximation creates a third space that is neither here nor there, but it is home for us.

8

Home is the white noise of the ocean and dried salt on my skin. Home is red rocks that must be climbed or swum around in order to continue along the beach. Home is fish, and deep fryers, and angry tourists who want to be served *now*. (A memory: seventeen years old, working at a fish 'n' chip shop. A tourist threw a Chiko Roll at my face because he insisted it wasn't fresh, even though I'd taken it out of the fryers myself just moments before.) Home is glaring sunlight, and sad, sulky, rained-in days, with bay winds and lightning shows across the water.

Home is souvenir shops and small businesses coming and going with the seasons. Home is long hours on the phone between towns, and a 45-minute bus ride to school. Home is checking out the rips on the way over the bridge connecting the island to the mainland, and watching rivulets join up and break apart to form the channel at different parts of the year.

There's a beach that stretches all the way around Phillip Island. 360 degrees. There are boulders, grasses and nettles, snakes, cliffs without access pathways – to circumnavigate the island you'd need to overcome all of these. And time – you would also need to overcome time. It would take a day or more to walk all the way around it. I'd recommend stopping in Rhyll, grabbing some fish and chips, camping overnight there because it's not too windy and the view of the horizon is uninterrupted.

But there's also that bridge off the island, connecting it to the mainland, and this is what kept me breathing when I lived there. With the beach wrapped around it, the island is claustrophobic but safe, and there is always an escape route. In a tourist town that's home to some 10 000 people off-season (when I lived there, around 8000), and 40 000 people on-season, everybody knows everybody else's business on Phillip Island.

Home is not being a surfer, but looking at the surf anyway on the way past Kilcunda bridge. Home is the menacing *wapwapwapwapwap* of plovers, the *whoosh* and swipe of their wings as they swoop into empty paddocks and nest in hidden corners of the primary school. Home is not fitting, but feeling safe enough anyway.

Home is a place that proves everything that built you. I can walk around Phillip Island and point out the spots where I became me. There, I had my first kiss. There, I broke my leg. There, I wrote FUCK on the toilet wall with a permanent marker on a dare (well, there, but no longer there – mid-air, mid-asphalt, hovering only in memory). There, I saw a doctor every few weeks as a teenager. There, my first job. There, embarrassment. There, pride. There understanding and there confusion.

Home can be a place; a town in which you know the people and what they stand for. It can be a building. I know people whose parents live in the house they grew up in, and who may very well inherit it when their parents die.

A home is a base of sorts. It's a reliable place that exists as a constant in your life – no matter what happens, you can always go home. Until you can't.

I moved away from the island by choice. I got older and wanted more – more space to spread my life out, more exposure to more people and ideas, more ability to become anonymous in a crowd of people and the freedom I imagined might come with such anonymity – and so I left. For a while I came home on weekends. Dad still owned and lived in the three-bedroom brick house we lived in while I was in high school, and Mum was in a small unit a few streets away. The scenery and people and attitudes were familiar. Reliable.

I woke in that house like I did often in my final years there, in the middle of the night. Our dog, Mac, snored at the foot of my bed.

Don't check the time; don't check the time; don't check the time.

I checked the time.

2 am. Only an hour and a half after I'd gone to bed.

I sent a message to the friend who lived across the road, who was a year younger than me, and part of the reliability I enjoyed in coming home. We went to different schools, but his friendship was a good part of that house. We met often still. Now I was old enough to drink wine with his mum when I visited. At least when I couldn't sleep on these weekends at home, I could check in with him.

U up?

We met on the road between our houses, the streetlights casting a glow on to the road between our abandoned beds.

This cul-de-sac was abandoned too at 2 am, and so we lay in the middle of the dim glow, looking up at the stars. Sometimes we spoke about what life is like when you go to the city; sometimes we hummed Simon & Garfunkel's 'Mrs Robinson' or 'Cecilia'; sometimes we just lay there comfortable in one another's company.

'We have a spare room in the share house. You should come live with me in the city' – this was on a night towards the end of his final school year, or perhaps in the new year soon after he'd finished.

He filled the spare room quickly, and the tenderness continued in the way we cared for one another when we still couldn't sleep, despite moving away from that place, and carrying each other's sense of home. *U awake* from across the hall instead of across the road. We lay perfectly still and I cried because I couldn't manage another night awake.

'You don't have to sleep', he said into the dark, 'but you do have to rest.' We stared at the ceiling until suddenly I was waking to our other housemate stomping down the hall.

This was a good summer, mostly – we pulled the TV on to the back porch and watched *The Young Ones* in a hammock. I experimented with styling his shaggy brown curls. He went without shoes most of the time. This was the way of things, until a dip – the dip I now recognise when it's coming, but I didn't recognise it then. It was how things went until he got sick, and I got sick, and he moved back, and soon after it all I attended his funeral in a church with dated yellow carpet; a church that had always been there, but one I'd never had cause to go into in all my seventeen years living close to it.

Then Dad sold the familiar house, and I no longer had a place that was my own to return to.

But Mum was still there. Her house wasn't one I'd grown up in, but she was still Mum, and it was still the island, and I was still welcome there. Whether I wanted to or not, I'd still run into people I knew, or who knew me, or some long-ago version of me, when I went to the supermarket. The island would often have changed on my return, the shock of not-my-town was too bizarre, making it in many ways unrecognisable. Pausing at traffic lights. Driving past a Subway. Mum would 'go to Safeway' and I'd think she meant the Safeway a 45-minute drive away, until I remembered that now there was one just two blocks away.

Then Mum left, too. It was a good leaving, hopeful. I'm glad she did. But now the part of the world where I grew up no longer has a house I can call home. There are very few familiar people there, and none of my relatives. When Mum left, even though I had myself left some nine years earlier, I felt cast adrift. My own little apartment in the city is the home-est home I have now. I have been renting it with my partner for five years. I do not, cannot, own it.

Now, when people who visit the island tell me about new buildings, improved infrastructure, a change in traffic management, I realise that they know more about my home town than I do.

I don't go to Phillip Island any more. Of course, I carry bits of it with me. Home *is* where the heart is, and my home exists in my memories; in the indentation of this place in the person I am now. In the fact that it is, largely, where I became who I am.

But when neither building nor geographical area are applicable concepts any more, where do I go to return 'home'?

I go to the dinner table. I go to the recipes we share – the spice rubs, the fruit cakes, the zucchini slices, the classics listed in the long-since-gone 'Kindy cook book' distributed as a kindergarten fundraiser. I go to the flavours that are tied to that place, even if there's nobody there any more who remembers them too. I go to the flavours that are tied to every other place we've gathered in. I go to the pantry, I go to the supermarket, I go to the stove. I bring plates and suggest restaurants and go about rebuilding a home with the people I love who have left, in this new space that is different but which still matters. We work at reconstructing home using the thing that has always brought us together: food.

9

Catholics believe that during Mass the communion bread and wine 'transubstantiate'. That is, the bread and wine's substance becomes the real body and blood of Christ. Catholics are blessed to receive and have something holy inside of them, and it brings them closer to God.

As a non-believer I should find this puzzling – it could fade into the inconceivable noise of a culture I'm not part of, as many religious rituals do. But this one doesn't. I think of the shared meals and food gifts that stabilise and fortify. I think of the comfort of a bowl of something warm. I think of reaching out for the foods that soothe sadness or stress.

I understand how food might be anything but what it appears to be.

10

There is aspiration in eating; consumption and nourishment are so full of possibility. This is such an easy story to find, hidden barely under the surface of the stories I (and probably you) grew up with. I start spotting the moments where food speaks, and it's almost impossible to stop.

Oliver Twist approaches his master with his bowl raised into the air. 'Please sir, I want some more.' Oliver has been nominated by the other boys, and asks for more because they want him to: it is a dare, a challenge. He isn't shy, he doesn't demur – 'I want some more'. But he's also not really asking for the food.

Mary Poppins' 'spoonful of sugar' is a metaphor for making horrible tasks more enjoyable through play. If the spoon had been full of actual sugar, I suspect Michael and Jane would have felt comforted and motivated all the same.

When Jo March pulls a luxurious pear from her new letterbox (a tiny house, which has been filled with food – perhaps the ultimate comfort), we love Laurie too. Even when Beth is dying, it's food that brings the warmth and softness. 'You drink up all that good broth', Jo says to her, spooning soup into her sister's mouth with all the care and tenderness in the world. She feeds Beth as if it can help stave off Death, who blows in through the window in just a second. As if all the good broth in the world could help at all.

Maria in *The Sound of Music* lists her favourite things, which include crisp apple strudel and schnitzel with noodles. It's not even the specific tastes – the memory of those things is enough. Maria's heart is breaking, her faith wavers, but she can always remember her favourite things.

These redemptive food stories are everywhere: Elizabeth Gilbert, carb-loading her way back into her body and her life. Lady and the Tramp chewing and slurping their shared spaghetti, culminating in that iconic kiss. Julie Powell following in Julia Child's footsteps, using attempted mastery of gourmet French cookery as a shield against all the uncontrollable things life keeps serving up.

Despite all the period costumes, dubbed voices and orchestral accompaniment (as well as the fact that some of these characters aren't even human), these films are so familiar to me, and I love them for that. I relate to them. They reflect the things I hope food will live up to, and sometimes it fulfils those hopes. This is what I am reaching for when I turn to food for comfort. In these films, and in many others, food stands as a shining beacon of wellness, happiness, togetherness. Or, at the very least, as a comfort against great hurt. Everywhere I look, someone tells me that food is an answer to almost anything: heartbreak, celebration, difficulty communicating. Food is presented as the saviour; the ultimate contentment and solace.

So many stories exist about what food means that it's impossible not to attach narratives to what we're eating: celebration food, conference food, workplace baking, family meal, eating alone, delivery food, comfort food, or *My sympathies* baked into a casserole, stored in the freezer for when grief is overwhelming. The weight of all these stories – of all these different ways of eating – means that of course, we expect to feel a particular way around food, and then reward or punish ourselves based on whether we're living up to these stories. These are the standards my disappointment is measured against, when food fails to meet my expectations. These are the stories I wish I could anchor myself in when food becomes something to worry over.

Food speaks. It intones – low, calm – *it'll be okay.*

11

It started, for me, as a question about why memory is so persistent around food; why all this significance hangs upon eating.

Or, well, no. That sounds short-sighted and clinical, and I know that this isn't where it *started*. Not really. Its starting point is less located in language, not a formulated or conscious question but something born in my body and in feeling. It starts in my skin. My memories of food live throughout my body; sometimes those pieces light up again in tasting – I taste with my hands, I taste with my eyes and ears. There is a link between my memory and my body: if it weren't for all this remembering, I might just fall apart.

It started in battle and it followed me home in the moments of respite – survivor's guilt.

My body, with its tingling extremities, its tingling centre – my body becomes alive with memory when I eat, and its starting point is my skin; that really quite flimsy membrane that sits between me and the world. Between what I am and what the world is. My body lets memory in, at the same time as it exudes memory – memories seem to come from both without and within. It's strange that sense memory doesn't start on my tongue – you'd think the taste buds would be the home of all food memories, but they're

73

not. It's the other things that mediate my experience in the world – my eyes (which see beautiful desserts and appreciate their architectural aspects), my nose (which transports smell, and with it the memory of one of Dad's workplaces when I smell lobster), my ears (burnt butter sounds like white noise), and my hands (the memory of making, serving, eating). My whole body is in. It's the hokey-pokey of the memory.

When I encounter mangoes, I am transported to the memory of climbing aboard a tram from the Queen Victoria Market to North Melbourne. I say 'encounter' because I'm not only talking about eating. This memory wakes up when I smell mangoes, or when I hold one in my palm. The memory rocks gently from side to side, and I feel the sun on my bare legs. I'm cupping a huge mango in my hand. I'm travelling home with my lover; the mangoes are an extension of our confident bodies. Then even further back, to porcupined mangoes, the bright flesh of the fruit sticking out at angles like puzzle pieces – evidence of my father's sure knife skills. Then back to the tram and the sun. Forward again, to the house in North Melbourne. The memory aches in my palms. They feel again the question-mark curve of hand against mango echoing the curve of hand against breast. The boldness of a fruit having such a large, single seed at its centre. We drank smoothies in bed. We drank up all the summer we could get. Drank one another. My fingers tingle with the sugary tack of mango juice. When I eat mangoes I remember tangled bedsheets.

My nose, my legs, the palms of my hands are all destined to appreciate mangoes; they're all part of the anticipation before the mango goes anywhere near my mouth.

Media and cultural studies academic Ben Highmore suggests that

> to concentrate on taste to the exclusion of other senses
> means to fail to recognize that the experience of eating
> is also dependent on the haptic sensitivity of tongues
> and mouths, and on sight and sound (the cacophony of
> crunching might actually be part of the 'flavor' of potato
> chips, for example).

The experience of flavour doesn't only live in the mouth, and so the memory of flavour must surely be elsewhere, too.

Perhaps memory itself is essential to flavour. Perhaps in eating comfort foods we're ingesting comfort as much as food. Studies have shown that 'comfort foods' are as comforting as they are because of their association with the loved ones who fed them to us, more so than any qualities inherent to the foods themselves.

Perhaps mangoes would taste different without the porcupine and the palm-cupping and the summer and the lover. Strawberry creams might just be cloyingly sweet without that gift from my brother.

But the problem with food is that it seems simple. It's something we have to interact with every day, and so might easily be taken for granted. It's so normal, so necessary, that we hardly think of it at all: it's just fuel; if you stop eating, you die.

But if it's a simple food-in-energy-out transaction,

then why can't I just eat a mango and have it be a delicious mango? Why are these mango memories so insistent in my body? The memory tingles on my face, in my palms, against my teeth.

When I eat, when I feel, when I crave – these are the times that my senses can become overwhelmed and memories bustle in. I remember particular foods, but I also remember all the stories that I have created around them. These memories come with attachments.

Mangoes are tied up in the push and pull of seasonal food, and the effects this has on my mood. They're too much part of the story of a particular summer, and of all the summers of my life.

In the first volume of Proust's *Remembrance of Things Past*, the narrator eats a madeleine with some tea, and is visited by memories of his life that he had previously thought were lost to him. The past holds the narrator's body captive, and memory is enacted through his senses, until he arrives at the conclusion that the memory doesn't *reside in* him, but rather that it *is* him. He relives the memory viscerally, from the inside out.

Anyone else, with the same tea and biscuit, would have remembered something entirely different – or nothing at all. Not all food feels tethered in this way.

Proust's narrator's memory isn't a prop or a thing locked away in the past. It *is* his very self. It is the reminders that swim up through all that's been and is present in his body. His body relives his memories – the shock of an unexpected memory, jostling in on a smell or sound or taste.

I think I have found a kindred eater and rememberer

in Proust and the narrator of *Remembrance of Things Past*.

I, too, am possessed and haunted by the past. I worry whether the writing of personal stories and memoir means that I look backward too much, too often, and search for meaning where there is none. But then, my guiding gut-feeling points back to the persistent question – isn't there meaning in everything that appears to me? Doesn't there have to be? And if these memories are so insistent, surely there's something in there. I'm not latching on to memory. Rather, memory latches on to me.

At the time, setting the table with my brother was nothing. It was a daily ritual, a chore. Nothing.

Now I dissect it. I poke at it until it speaks, and insist that it has something to say. Writing down is a process of learning the language that my memories favour.

And while it's comforting to think of pinning down memory through language, it's also baffling. Understanding how my memories come back doesn't do much to explain *why*. It doesn't unravel this tangle of eating and remembering.

Dutifully, I recreate my mind for the page, creating chains from it. I weave, stitch, tie, follow. Chase.

But also, this: my memories are fizzly fireworks. They shoot skyward, driven by quiet energy, and then explode in all directions. Sometimes the colours change. Sometimes there's a third or fourth explosion on the way down. Sometimes they're an underwhelming little dot that looks like it might turn into something beautiful, but just squiggles away into the night in almost-silence: pfffff-nothing.

12

Raspberries bring me memories of my maternal grandparents. Raspberry memories sit on the edges of my tongue, and are called up in the sweet tang of summer, when they're relatively cheap at $4.50 a punnet. Raspberries are tiny canyons glittering with jewels – to eat them is to swallow wealth.

Oma and Opa's gardens on the properties where they lived in Tasmania have always been things of wonder. Market gardening left them skilled at raising almost anything from a patch of soil; this was particularly true of Opa. At my own childhood home we grew mint, sunflowers and cherry tomatoes – the kinds of plants that do well when left mainly untended. Mum loved growing roses, and Dad loved to prune them, but you can't make a whole meal out of roses. Mum loves jonquils when they peek out of the springtime ground, but they always seem to be something of a surprise: a bulb that gives and gives, but is forgotten between seasons. The soil at home felt and often looked like clay. Oma and Opa's carefully tended garden, and the ritual of harvesting and eating, was entirely different – my grandparents' veggie patch was an enduring kindness and source of plenty.

The first property of theirs I remember visiting had land and crops, and they supplied local greengrocers from their market garden – my grandfather's Dutch carrots earned him the nickname of 'the Carrot King'. As my grandparents downsized houses over the years, their gardens got smaller. Oma is now by herself after Opa's death, living in a unit with small, raised garden beds on the front lawn. This seems like the truest indicator of her ageing that I've seen yet, and the most final goodbye to my grandfather.

As a child I crouched low against the prickly mulch of my grandparents' berry patch. Raspberries were my favourite. If the berry was ripe, the fruit gave way and the plant sprang back into place. Even in the months when the Tasmanian frost meant there were no raspberries for me to pick, I could always enjoy their flavour in Oma's raspberry sauce, which she made during raspberry season in large batches and set aside in the pantry for later months. The sauce was used for desserts, and was sent home in our backpacks, nestled between clothes to guard against breakage. We took that taste of Tasmania and our grandparents' love home with us.

'Are you finished?' Oma asked at the end of a meal, her voice lilting as only a migrant's can – the rhythm and inflection of a mother tongue patched imprecisely on to English. She clicked her tongue, picking up my spoon and the bowl I'd thought was empty. As she whisked the spoon around the edge, her raspberry sauce and homebrand ice cream materialised – two whole tablespoons appeared from nowhere, like fairy floss appearing to be spun from nothing but air.

My grandparents' stories are shards of light through a half-open doorway.

Opa was afraid of horses, and it had something to do with the war. I think I heard this in a kitchen, looking out over a paddock. Whenever it was, I pictured Opa, a frightened boy, in Holland. I pictured horses rearing, and soldiers. These images appeared in my mind like old photographs, frozen or stuttering in sepia tones. The only things I know are true here are 'horses' and 'war'. I cannot explain the rest. There's so much that my family don't talk about, so much so that even impersonal, not-present, abstract horses seem too much.

At eighteen months old, I could fit comfortably under the benches in my grandparents' sheds. Opa stood at the bench washing carrots. The bifurcated ones – those that look like people with two or more legs, whose single root had hit a bump during their growth and split in the soil – were thrown aside for the cows to eat. The rest of the carrots were perfect stems with small curves or bumps, and with tiny hairs and a stretching root that looked as though it could keep growing indefinitely. Delicate foliage stretched out at the carrots' tops, with parsley-looking fronds luxuriating in a dainty sag.

Under the bench, water dripped between the slats. Light poured through the massive rolling tin doors, thrown open despite the chill. Opa whistled and hummed, and I laughed. The smell of carrots was everywhere – the smell of fresh carrots now brings back the song I sang that day. I had let it tumble out in a high-pitched blurt, 'Opaaaa, ha-haaa, ha-ha!', and across the years this little ditty somehow became a central part of the connection between my grandfather and me. He hummed it to me the last time we saw one another, and when he did, our now and our then pulled close for a second as though attached by string. The distance between who we had been and who we had become seemed nothing – we might have looked older, frailer, but we were still the same.

Another day, in another kitchen, I was told about Opa's only work shirt freezing on the washing line in the Dutch winter. I was told about the time he jumped into a lake to save my grandmother from drowning after she refused to admit she couldn't swim. I was told about the packages of biscuits that came in rations during the war, which Oma's mother made into porridge. I made the connection between these fragments of a foreign place and my grandparents, but only in a roundabout way – 'then' seems so distant. I wanted my idea of my grandparents to be filled out by their stories, but instead it fractured. They seemed to have lived so many different lives.

When I was writing Opa's eulogy, Mum handed me a list of notes about his life. There were so many little details I didn't really know: the boat trip to Australia took four weeks. He sold his first head of lettuce for 10 cents. He bought and renovated fifteen houses, and with each move, his spade was the last thing on to the removal truck and the first thing off, so he could test the soil. He'd be pulling vegetables from the dirt within weeks.

I copied Mum's notes, including 'He tried his hand at farming'. Rethinking this, Mum asked me to remove it from the eulogy. They had done their farming at the property where one of my uncles, who I never met, took his own life.

And we don't talk about that.

We don't talk about it, and still … I feel it in my body and it is something I know without entirely understanding. I feel it in my experience of my mother's never-entirely-mended mental health, in the ever-present terror of losing my loved ones, in the tight shoulders of hypervigilance. Watching; waiting; and under it all, grief. We don't speak of it, but my uncle's suicide is always present, and always a cause for everything that came after. This is not my experience: not one I own, but one I inherited. Unspoken, unknown, but held in my body.

Recently reading memoirist Meera Atkinson's *Traumata*, I have come to think differently about the ways trauma is passed along community and family lines. In particular, Atkinson cites literary scholar Marianne Hirsch's idea of 'postmemory'. I follow the thread to Hirsch's work, and this idea hits home with my knowledge of my uncle, and the lives that came before mine:

> Postmemory's connection to the past is thus not actually mediated by recall but by imaginative investment, projection, and creation. To grow up with such overwhelming inherited memories, to be dominated by narratives that preceded one's birth or one's consciousness, is to risk having one's own stories and experiences displaced, even evacuated, by those of a previous generation. It is to be shaped, however indirectly, by traumatic events that still defy narrative reconstruction and exceed comprehension. These events happened in the past, but their effects continue into the present.

So my family speak only around the edges of experience, but one thing that's always included is that my grandfather was born to make things grow. Before his casket was lowered into the ground, our family placed Dutch carrots on top in a final gesture of farewell, and it seemed right.

In the years before he died, Opa had begun to forget – he remembered things from a long time ago with perfect clarity, but his logic for the present was scrambled. He talked to me more often in Dutch, and while I only understood snippets, I knew we were glad to be around one another. He still enjoyed his food, especially the sweet things. We shared dessert after dinner – apple crumble with ice cream. He had just a spoonful of crumble and a mound of ice cream. He still told stories from his days market gardening, about supermarket orders that arrived late, so that he and Oma had to pull spring onions from the earth at 3 am to fill the order on time. His hands were gnarled from twisting carrot tops for all those years. As he shared his stories, his mind might meander, and Oma was always there with the detail that set things right again. Together, they lined up their lives for us behind those memories of strength and endurance.

But on one of my last visits I watched him peel his afternoon apple slowly, and when he dropped the plate of peelings, he stared at it on the floor. I was unsure whether he'd pick it up. My concept of my Opa didn't include this old man who needed my help. Months before he died, Mum rang to tell me they'd removed the second hand from Opa's watch, because it confused him. In the end, Opa lost time constantly.

The earthen smell of carrots makes me hum, and the tart zap of raspberries reminds me to clean my plate properly. I think of Oma and Opa's pantry full of preserves, tall jars of raspberry sauce shimmering in neat rows, the freezer stacked full with blanched vegetables from the garden. I can't imagine Opa or Oma ever not having enough. Rather, my memories involve their *creating* enough, whether it was there to begin with or not – pulling something from nothing. Stretching wartime rations out to an extra portion, or raising raspberries from the dirt. They have always pulled 'enough' from nowhere and made it real for us.

'My dinner was noble and enough', says Samuel Pepys in *The Joys of Excess*. It's hard to tell whether this seventeenth-century diarist and politician is glad for 'enough', or whether he's saying it's nothing special. In Pepys' time, choice was rather more limited, but the prospect of a dinner that's 'enough' does seem worth celebrating – that we ever have enough at all is something of a miracle, though that's so easy to forget when I'm surrounded every day by so very much: so overwhelmed by choice and availability.

My family lean away from difficult stories and focus instead on how to properly clean a plate. How to wash carrots in the early morning Tasmanian frost. How to pick a raspberry.

13

Christmas time when I was a kid was a rare opportunity to peek into Dad's restaurant life. Usually all I saw were aluminium take-away containers with paper lids; the leftovers of whatever he'd had for dinner. There remained an aura; the smell of cracked and peeled seafood. The appearance of cuts and burns on Dad's hands. My knowledge of Dad's job – perhaps of Dad at all during that time – lived in the spaces of his absence: our fridge, our kitchen bench, the sound of his sleeping, my mother saying, *I'll have to tell your father*.

At the restaurant where Dad worked during my primary school years, my Grade 2 class visited the kitchen as a school excursion. As a fancy seafood restaurant in a beachside town, it was a popular destination for both tourists and locals. On the excursion day, Dad took the class to see the lobster tank, an enormous round swimming pool in a wooden building out the back of the restaurant. The lobsters were moved from this tank into the smaller fish tanks downstairs where diners could choose the one they wanted.

My school group walked up the metal stairs (reminiscent of New York–style fire escapes, where in movies the bad guys run away, or the secret lovers sneak, missing a shoe, into the night). When we reached the landing, I turned left, towards the office, which smelled like freshly pressed jackets and Dad. Lobsters were funny little creatures, but ones I could conceive of, so the tanks held no wonder for me. My father's life, on the other hand, was a fascinating unknown – my imagination was fuelled by the glimpses I had caught, by unfamiliar smells, and by the inkling knowledge that if you have something you treasure and want to keep for yourself, you put it in a room behind a door and you don't invite anyone in there. You keep it secret and safe.

I wanted to know what was in that office.

In my mind, Dad's world at the restaurant was sparkly and unique. I wanted to show this to my classmates, to hint at and be appreciated for its secrecy and foreignness: the unknowability of it all. *What's impressive here is not the size of the pots and pans, or the sealife, but the way you can almost connect with your actual dad in this place!* But we didn't go into the office that day, we turned right to the lobster tanks. As Dad pulled open the door, and everyone 'ooh'ed' at the size of the pools, I gave up on the office and pretended I found the lobsters interesting.

At home, it was only on Christmas Day that I really got an idea of what Dad did for a job.

At Christmas lunch we sat around an elaborate table, and ate crab, lobster, and prawns. We piled our plates high.

This scene strikes me now as a very neat 'before' picture – before Dad burnt out and decided to leave the restaurant, before Mum became sick on a regular basis, before our family income and dynamic changed significantly. Seafood at Christmas time: before.

I didn't like the way the prawns' beady eyes stared at

me, and their feelers stretched out, seeking. Attempting to tackle lobster, I would fumble and stab myself on the barbed shells. These animals' defence mechanisms against being eaten were quite persuasive, but still, we'd won. There they lay as part of our Christmas spread. Dad peeled my seafood for me. In this small moment, handing my father an unruly prawn, he is there, and playing the protective father role.

In the lazy hours between ripping the paper from presents and our lunchtime feast, my parents had made a huge plate of Dutch potato salad. The vinegar zap and little squares of apple make it unique – I don't properly enjoy Australian potato salad; to me it tastes heavy and one-dimensional. For our Christmas dish, I helped by preparing the tiny gherkins and pickled cocktail onions; fiddly work that I enjoyed. The little onions scattered away under my grip, but I thinly sliced the gherkin and felt satisfied when I finished, left with a bowl of strange green confetti. From the kitchen I could hear Dad snoring on the couch. In the afternoon, when the excitement had died down, we all might take a nap. The house would fall silent for a moment.

But before that was the meal. Preparing lunch, we sculpted the salad into a perfect dome before decorating it with pieces of gherkin and onion in elaborate patterns. Sitting down at the table together, looking at our feast, that moment was the kind of theatre my family and I all enjoy in our food. The theatricality of that Christmas meal – all of our efforts at putting it together, each playing a part in what we could then share together – this was the drum roll and 'ta-dah' that keeps us coming back, and that keeps us giving food to one another over all these years, in the hope of a 'wow'.

Christmases are different now, as an adult. Perhaps they are for everyone – perhaps the magic of Christmas just quietens over the years until it's simply another day. Or perhaps it's something about the shift in my own family's proximity to one another. Christmases now are held at different tables in different houses. I'm surrounded by different family – family I didn't even know would be mine when I was a kid. These are my partner's people, my step-mum's people. Or even further out; the people of those people. Food gifts at Christmas hold on to an important part of what we no longer do as our family of four; although it's a new tradition, exchanging preserves and biscuits make Christmas a little less strange.

At Christmas with my step-mum's Maltese family, the food is plentiful and good: pasties filled with steaming, salty corned beef; fluffy pastry pastizzi whose golden crusts fracture and spill down the front of my shirt; desserts of banoffee pie and blondies and always cannoli with its piped creamy centre in different flavours. Here I have been embraced, and always made to feel welcome. Nonetheless, this new family Christmas doesn't quite match my childhood Christmas rhythm – it's taken some years to get used to dining at a different family table. There's no napping in the afternoon; no potato salad with gherkin confetti.

For a number of years, when these step-family Christmases were new, on Christmas Eve I would arrange jars of preserves and home-baked goods into baskets and wrap them with cellophane. In their respective houses, my dad and step-mum and my brother were doing the same. For one night, my pantry would be depleted: maybe a single, stray jar of kumquat jam or preserved lemons standing alone. By the following evening the pantry overflowed again with jams and preserves from my family, as we tried to out-preserve one another again for Christmas. Proving we cared the most, had the most love to give, by squeezing it into jars. A global food preservation project from Tessa Zettel (of Sydney art collective Makeshift) called this 'making time' – observing both the stretchy quality of time spent preserving food (sterilising, boiling slowly, watching for the set point), and preserving's ability to capture time in a jar by pausing a moment of plenty and locking it safely away. The giving of preserves within my family is a new kind of tradition; one we've shared even while we're surrounded by strange Christmas rituals. When we hand over our jars and packets it creates a small piece of quiet like that we shared in the old years.

Christmas now is a constant negotiation. (*Are you my Christmas?*) We pile new ways up, expanding the possibilities for what Christmas might be. We fill the empty space with what comfort we can. We stockpile it in our pantries for the long year.

The explosive theatre of it all is so seductive. So precious. *Gezellig*.

14

I assumed that eating was the default activity for all families, but as I've grown older and spent time with other families, this has come to seem less true. Sometimes families resort to pranks. Sometimes families tease or joke or get drunk. The default for some other families is anger or silence, or noise. For my own family, it's food and eating.

'What would we do without all this food to bring us together?' my step-mum recently asked me. I wouldn't know where to start.

—

In the evenings of my childhood, I watched my mother prepare the nightly meal. She stood over the bench, shifting on her feet periodically, patience visible in the pop of her hip, the way she stood in place, and her concentration. She diced chicken into 3-centimetre cubes and sat it in a bowl in front of her. In another dish filled with water, bamboo skewers floated like miniature rafts. She worked methodically and with purpose. Her weaving and threading was hypnotic, like work at a loom. My mother is a crafter, and when she's knee-deep in a project, the rhythm and logic of the making takes hold. She brought this sensibility even to the threading of chicken skewers.

Cubes of chicken stacked up until the skewer was full, and then she began the next. After enough skewers were made for the three or four of us, they'd go into a hot frying pan – not hot enough to make the chicken seize up, but enough to cook the small cubes and give them colour, a light caramelisation on the outside.

The cooked chicken skewers would be slathered with Mum's thick, peanut buttery sauce. Salty and just a little bit sweet, with small, crunchy chunks of peanut peppered throughout. Sometimes there was pineapple in it, providing a tiny bomb of acidity and sweet canning syrup. Mum's satay sauce wasn't particularly spicy, which is probably why we liked it so much as kids. If I had to guess now how Mum made that sauce, I might think something about Kraft (now Bega) crunchy peanut butter and Maggi seasoning, but this is imprecise. Its exact composition is still a mystery to me, and possibly will be forever, but it's a flavour I'm on the lookout for, always.

—

In *First Bite: How we learn to eat*, British food writer Bee Wilson calls attention to the ways we glean food preferences and habits from those around us – none of us learns in isolation, and the specifics of eating, as with so many other acts that make us human, are learned.

Sure, we eat for sustenance. But what and how we eat – that's social. At the dining room table we become who we are, and learn who we will be. The self becomes known in relation to the bodies it sits alongside at mealtimes.

'Eating is not something we are born instinctively knowing how to do, like breathing', says Wilson. 'It is *something we learn*. A parent feeding a baby is training him or her how food should taste.'

Wilson goes on to suggest that we learn to eat before we reach the family table at all – before we even leave our mothers' bodies. We might assume that at least the very first sustenance we come in contact with – that is, what reaches us in the womb from our mothers' diets, wending through our mothers' bodies and delivered as essential nutrition through the umbilical cord – is something all of us have in common, but as Wilson points out, even the way children are nourished in the womb affects the eating habits they form later. Garlic in the diet can be detected in amniotic fluid, and babies whose mothers' diets were high in garlic are more likely to prefer garlicky foods later in life. These babies would fit right into their garlic-loving families, so that their flavour preferences give them a better chance at survival, too.

Social factors are significant: in the sixteenth century, colostrum – the nutrient-dense breastmilk first produced by a mammal – was viewed as too rich and ultimately harmful to babies. Closer to home, too: in 2015, celebrity chef Pete Evans hit controversy when his co-authored book *Bubba Yum Yum: The paleo way* encouraged parents to feed newborns a 'DIY baby milk formula' comprising a 'bone broth' derived from chicken livers and containing an amount of vitamin A that the Public Health Association of Australia claimed was unsafe for babies. The book's publisher, Pan Macmillan, scrapped it and Evans self-published instead.

A distrust of breastmilk echoes a general distrust of the body. It recognises that sometimes (many times) our bodies let us down. Besides this, there's some strange misogyny at work here: the incredible masculinity of a paleo diet is one thing (bringing to mind muscle-building, meat-eating, protein fetishists), but ruling out breastmilk says that women's bodies can't produce the right stuff, despite housing, nourishing and growing the child who would receive the milk.

Wilson also cites studies of breastfeeding mothers and their children's food preferences once weaned. Babies whose breastfeeding mothers consumed anise or carrots preferred the flavours they already knew when it came time to move on from breastmilk.

Babies are sometimes born with 'sucking blisters' – small blisters on the lips, hands or arms created by sucking while still in the womb. Those same lips that will be used to cry out, the same arms and hands to reach and hold.

—

My brother Chris has tried to recreate Mum's satay sauce at home. He knows more than I do about recreating dishes, not just from guessing at flavour combinations, but because he understands the science of food. He gets the how and why of food reactions – he knows why the texture of Mum's satay was thick but also velvety. He knows how to recreate the salt level without it tasting too much of soy sauce or table salt. He has trained over stovetops and at benches and with whisks and ladles and knives. But even in his kitchen, with all his expertise, my brother hasn't recreated Mum's satay in a way that he finds satisfactory.

I have taken too many chances on the wrong satays. There are satays I regret – not bad satays, but not the *right* satays. Satays that are too thin, or don't contain chunks of peanut, or are more fish sauce or paste based than peanut-butter based. There are so many satays in the world that are not my mother's satay.

It's a catch-22. I can find satay on a menu and order it, running the risk of disappointment because it doesn't live up to my memory of the satays that I've eaten at Mum's table. Or I can find satay on a menu and avoid ordering it, because I know already that it will never be my mum's satay. But if I don't order the satay, I'll never find the satay. I just want to go out for dinner and be served this dish that Mum made for me and that I love. I want the world's satay – whether that's genuine satay or 'the right way' to make satay or if it's just Mum's peanut-butter approximation – to live up to my childhood table memories.

—

Everyone knows their parents' food first and best. At some point, for most of us, food and our mothers' bodies were synonymous. As we grew, we graduated from womb to boob or bottle to table, and the foods that our parents cooked for us created an imprint. Soon enough we have our own kitchens, and we do the cooking and the passing-along ourselves. To our own families, perhaps, but also to our friends, housemates, romantic partners. We recreate the flavours we know and love.

My mum cooked the dinners for most of my childhood, and so her food tastes like home. Nothing special, just home. Just home – just everything.

As children we develop patterns and taste preferences that remain, always. We are taught how to eat. Like a needle follows a record's spiral groove, we move towards familiar flavours throughout our lives. Even when we seek out something different, it's different in reference to this baseline of the foods we grew up eating.

—

What I saw as home food, for the longest time, was Mum's small, reliable repertoire. Chicken satay, chow mein, chicken à la king, osso bucco, apricot chicken (I am only now recognising just how much chicken we ate – what spectacularly cheap and readily available protein!), meat with cauliflower, carrots and peas. Mum was dutiful about cooking, just as she was dutiful about the housework, though I imagine neither were the things she'd have wanted to be doing if given the choice. Walking into the kitchen each afternoon there would be pots and pans with peeled and cut-up vegetables, ready for the evening meal. Ready for the part of the day when Mum would bring our meat-and-three-veg together, and we would sit at our dining room table to share a meal. Cooking didn't seem like a particularly pleasurable or relaxing task for her, but at the same time, dinner was never rushed or thrown together.

When we sat together, I ate slowly, and my family would sit and wait until I was finished. I was fussy – I picked up each individual pea or corn kernel and peeled its shell away, or extracted sausage from its casing. I pulled my food apart – but can't tell you why, now. I cannot remember my motivation at all, but I do remember the rest of the family having to stay at the table until I'd finished my meal, and the groans my brother made. But eating as a family each night was important, so we'd all sit there until I was done.

Was I fussing to set myself apart? Was I fussing because there was something about those particular foods that unsettled me, and which was corrected by removing their outsides? Or was I just keeping my family at the dinner table with me for as long as I could? Am I still?

I don't remember thinking anything about Mum's food at the time – it was just the way we ate, just as so much of what happens around us as children seems natural, inevitable. Now, as someone who prepares meals for myself and my partner, I admire that Mum made it happen without any fuss every night of the week – or that it at least appeared this way to me. I feel, too often, like deciding what to eat is a chore or responsibility. Half the time I cook for pleasure. Half the time I would rather throw myself out the window than make another fucking meal. But my work hours are better, I work from home half the time, I am able to take pleasure in cooking when the mundanity doesn't get the better of me. And I guess, to an extent, that I'm living out all the gender stuff, which can be so hard to shrug off. Sometimes the responsibility of feeding us drags my heart through my body and out my feet, and I want to walk away, leaving it there on the kitchen floor.

Mum's food was both remarkable and unremarkable:

it was consistent, it was there, it was just how we ate. It was meal, after meal, after meal, after meal.

—

With Dad, the pattern has been much the same as with the rest of my family: eating together is our default mode of spending time in one another's company. Once, when I was about six years old, he took me into work with him because I was sick and Mum was working in childcare or cleaning, too. It was stock-take day, and Dad lugged huge piles of food out of the walk-in fridges and freezers, placing the piles on the floor outside. He carried a clipboard and marked down what was there before loading it all back in.

That day, as Dad counted the stock, he took out a 15-litre container. Nothing in the commercial kitchen was in the containers you would expect; things like mayonnaise vats got recycled as stock containers, and this meant that labels could not be trusted. On the stock-take sick day he gave me an ice cream container full of home-made honeycomb.

'I can't be bothered counting it.' Dad gave me a sly wink. 'Better eat it!'

So we sat down next to the fridge and ate the squeaky, sweet honeycomb together.

He, too, couldn't have me there and not feed me, because feeding is what you do with and for your loved ones.

15

'Pick anything you want, we'll make it together', Dad said to me. There was nothing he couldn't make, no recipe he wasn't willing to try out. My heart leapt in anticipation. Excitement bubbled in my throat.

If Mum's food was everyday, Dad's food was a special event.

Dad and I had made butterscotch, Turkish delight and toffee together before – sweets were the most magical, and the most scientific things in the kitchen. I continued to flip through the *Women's Weekly* cookbook, admiring the heaped piles of food – especially the sweets. The very high melting point of sugar meant that Dad was guiding me here through dangerous, grown-up territory. We piled ingredients into the sturdy Kenwood mixer. We hung over the bench, utterly still, watching the sugar thermometer until it reached its mark, and then we rushed on to the next step. The viscous smell of melting sugar floated above our heads. Sweets recipes were alchemy – part cooking, part magic trick.

The fact that these cooking-together memories stand out to me now says something about the rhythm of my relationship with Dad. I defined (still define) my father in terms of his connection to food. He was often away with food – at work, cooking because he loved to, and cooking to earn money because he loved *us* – or else at home but sleeping off the exhaustion of long days and weeks in the kitchen. He was at home with food – I don't remember him *teaching* me to cook, but I do remember us cooking together. His animation and confidence in the kitchen are now me, mine, my kitchen.

'Marshmallows?' – I half-whispered this, not truly believing that we might be able to create our own saccharine slabs of pillowy fluff.

The alchemy in marshmallows comes from gelatine. The leaves would always come out of the packet broken, and Dad would put them into a bowl of warm water, gently. The stiff, clear sheets seemed to disappear, as though they had just relaxed and given themselves over to our pursuit of the delicious.

'We'll let that go', Dad said, turning to the sugar and water, watching them dissolve too. Coming back to the gelatine bowl once it had softened, we added it to the sugar mix and turned the Kenwood mixer dial up, up, up. We shouted over the din, and I watched the mixture turn white and stiff. When we stopped it and pulled the blade out, we found fluffy cloud peaks.

On a huge biscuit tray (as wide as our oven, but not very deep) we poured out most of a packet of flour.

'We use the wide end so they're nice and big', Dad said, pressing an egg into the flour, creating divots where we poured marshmallow mixture. I thought of my friends, and knew that they didn't get to do this on weekends with their parents. I would bet money that they didn't have sugar thermometers, or a mixer as loud as a truck, or a dad who let them pick the recipe.

In Seamus Heaney's poem 'When all the others were away at Mass', the poet recalls the closeness of peeling potatoes alone with his mother. He describes the calm quiet of their focus – 'I remembered her head bent towards my head / Her breath in mine, our fluent dipping knives'. Heaney's body and his mother's echo one another in something as minute as the tilt of their heads; it leaves them 'never closer the whole rest of our lives'. This poem sits in my mind alongside the memory of making marshmallows with Dad.

We waited until the marshmallows had set before we flipped the little domes over and covered the bottom in flour, too. Rows and rows of divots and domes. Dad's wide hands measuring and mixing. Standing close to him against the bench. Building a memory together.

16

Epicurus has been misunderstood. He's often read as advocating for excessive and extravagant food; abandoning control in favour of decadence and fine fare. The thesaurus lists 'hedonistic' and 'self-indulgent' as synonyms for 'epicurean'. We've strayed from what that ancient Greek philosopher valued most.

What he really said was: let's eat together. Pass me the bread, and when I take it from you our hands touch. What mattered to Epicurus was this touch, the proximity of other people, the shared space and time.

I have square hands like Dad, with rounded, strong nails like Mum. My brother's hands are the opposite; he has rounder palms with wider, flatter nails. Our hands speak a little of the genetic lottery by which people inherit traits from their parents. If only all traits could be so easily identified.

My brother and I used to set the table together. We were given pocket money for carrying out our chores, like taking out the compost, setting the table or washing the dishes. It was our responsibility to stack and unstack the dishwasher, for those few glorious years when we had one.

Every night we would set the table with fork on the left, knife on the right, and spoon lying horizontally across the top of the plate. We took armfuls of condiments (never 'sauces', always 'condiments') out of the fridge and created a landscape with them in the middle of the table. Short jars and tall bottles. We prayed before dinner every night, for Mum. We never asked why, it was just part of our evening meal, something attached to Mum's upbringing that we had inherited.

'Our Father, who art in heaven …'

Before partaking in our daily bread, we bowed our heads and folded our hands, fingers laced, elbows resting on the table top. My brother prayed like a race call, fitting the whole Lord's Prayer into one breath; just a ten-second blurt before diving for the plate.

Markers like these remind me of home: square-set cutlery for dinner, sandwich buffets on weekends, prayers before a meal. Placing, reaching, clasping, passing.

Place a different family around our table, and it changes entirely. I was lucky to have that table as the centre of our family universe for so many years. It was unique, and I wish I could return to it. But the table itself is now long since sold or sent to landfill, and the family that once sat around it each now convene their own, different, new tables. And we are reconsidering the idea of our family table and what it means.

Maybe growing up is just trading in or upgrading the old furniture. Maybe it's learning to build your own, and inviting loved ones to join you at it.

17

Slowly my jaw begins to loosen. I feel a bit like *The Wizard of Oz*'s Tin Man, when Dorothy stumbles upon the frozen figure in the woods, as she picks apples up from the ground. Standing to meet the metal man's gaze, she oils his joints, starting with his mouth, and he says 'Mah, mah … my goodness, I can talk again!'. When she oils his arm, it drops and he lets out a sigh it's clear he's been holding ever since he rusted solid there in the woods a little over a year ago. It doesn't happen immediately, but I come to realise that I have been frozen solid for some time – too afraid to own my story or to speak out of turn in case I hurt someone or break something precious. But once I start … *My goodness. I can talk again.*

My mouth becomes unstuck, my tongue begins to flex and move. Words form from the air that moves up, out of my lungs. I start with the stories I am sure of, and move slowly to those I've shared less. I eye them off warily. I try to light up the hazy and uncertain memories. I try to pin down and interrogate. These words work hard, now that my jaw moves freely. They are intentional and they earn their space in the world.

18

I've heard that even when a tongue isn't doing anything, it is still active – because a truly flaccid tongue would fall down your throat and restrict your ability to breathe, choking you to death. To have a tongue in a living body necessitates its *doing* something, even when it is doing nothing, and there is so very much for a tongue to do.

Tongues for kissing. Tongues for licking the lips and teeth. Yours. Another's. Tongues for exploration. Tongues for connection.

—

Writing so honestly of my feelings about food brings an element of risk with it. There's a danger I might choke. This writing is risky, threatening blurred boundaries, and I can't help but see the danger in clambering over all I've internalised and committed to obey.

As a thing with defined borders (like skin), and further borders within those borders (those we're socialised to recognise) that we dare not trespass against, it's particularly tough to write the body in an open, curious, and freeing way. In attempting to write my own body, I constantly bump up against roadblocks – attitudes I dare not bend, taboos I fear to breach, assumptions I need to acknowledge before I can move past them and into something meaningful. It's confronting territory, and possibly the highest stakes thing to write about – that vehicle that allows a person to *be*. The body as wall, as barrier, as boundary. The body as the country you may not leave; you may not elect citizenship elsewhere, may not visit elsewhere, may not even pick up a brochure for elsewhere – elsewhere doesn't exist. The body is a kind of fate, for which you have always been destined, and to which you will always return.

At the same time, the body is also the thing we're most encouraged to deny exists. Your bodily reality must, at all costs, be disappeared. If you cannot manage this, then shame on you.

—

There's a sexy duplicity to eating tongue, and it feels risky to admit this. The fleshiness of tongue; the tender press of two organs used for tasting. It's almost obscene.

Tongue isn't sexy before it reaches my plate. Tongue, when first butchered out of an animal, looks as obvious as can be. Shocking in its length, its girth – a powerful muscle reduced to thick, fat nothing. Just looking at tongue makes my own tongue feel swollen and restricted. This is the kind of strong reaction many people feel when faced with the idea of eating offal.

The word 'offal' describes the non-muscle or bone parts that are often discarded – or, in Australia's case, exported – after the desirable cuts of meat have all been butchered.

Offal includes tongue, feet, head and snout, as well as vis-cera – kidney, liver, intestine, heart, pancreas and more. While these meats have been common fare on Australian plates in the past, they've gone out of favour more recently. We've gradually lost our taste for them, until, all of a sudden, offal seems beyond us.

Some cultures view offal as equal with any other piece of meat, while others still see offal as a delicacy due to its relative rarity – you can get multiple steaks from one cow, but only one brain, after all. Australians, however, are part of a culture that disdains offal – enamoured with good old muscle meats, many of us find it challenging to get around the idea of eating organs and offcuts. While offal isn't entirely taboo, its unfamiliar smells, textures and particu-lar preparations make people reluctant to make it a normal part of their diet.

—

In general, our food culture is very selective about what is acceptably tasty. We fuss about following food trends, favouring the particular and novel over the available – and there is so much good food available. We'd just rather Nutella-stuffed carbs, and at times this is good food too. In a climate where we're fortunate to have access to plenty of reasonably priced, high-quality food, we easily forget that, globally (and locally), not everyone is in the same boat. Food trends, on the whole, can be socially and ethically questionable. The human and environmental energy that goes into farming kale, for example, cannot be replaced as quickly as a food trend passes. The decline of food trends puts those who produce it out of business. Food trends are often also prohibitively expensive – the price gap between a plain cinnamon donut from the supermarket and a cronut, for example, means that the two are most often consumed by different people. To be seen eating either carries a vastly different message. Of course, there is trickle-down, as there was with chocolate lava cake. The oozy-centred cake eaten exclusively in fine-dining restaurants in late-1980s America is now available in microwavable pudding cups all over the world.

Where most food trends rely on the performance of status inherent in indulging particular tastes, consuming offal falls under the socially conscious banner of 'nose-to-tail eating'. This approach to cooking and consumption makes use of every part of the animal, discarding nothing. While the word 'offal' itself doesn't have diners flocking to tables, 'nose-to-tail eating' is a buzz phrase, helping offal find its way back on to our plates. Nose-to-tail converts only account for a small portion of the population though – the reality of eating an animal in its entirety is still a confronting idea for most.

Conversations about meat-eating in general tend to make people uncomfortable. They get defensive, and often flee to either end of an extreme argument: we love meat or we don't eat it at all. To love it often means to avoid looking at how it's produced, or to execute some strange double-think around what's going into our mouths. This is supported by the stories we're fed (where meat is a product, not a being; where the lives of animals are 'happy' – as if that's a meaningful term that could be measured), and the language we use (where the tray of meat in my hand is labelled 'steak', 'venison', or 'stir-fry strips'; when what was once 'sealife' transmogrifies into 'seafood'). But at its core, it's an ethical question – one which involves asking whether we can live with the slaughter and consumption of something that shares some aspects of its lived experience with humans: living, breathing, with a brain and blood.

Beyond this basic commonality, it's unclear what can be absolutely proven. The stories we tell about meat swing towards all or nothing. Either animals share too much with us (anthropomorphism) or nothing at all (in which case they're *too* different; why even bother worrying about their welfare?).

To eat meat is to make a decision, the significance of which forces us to contend with some confronting ethical questions. In this case, as in so many others, not making a decision (conscious or otherwise) counts as a decision. It means being implicated in a broken industry.

What if we backed away from polar opposites and accepted the idea of 'figuring it out'? If I don't want to be vegan, but decide instead to reconsider the architecture of my plate (so that meat accounts for a smaller portion of it), or only to eat meat when I can afford ethically produced products, isn't that still something? Isn't 'better' better than 'bad'?

Might this not include slowing down, being mindful, grateful, and respecting the whole body that has, in whatever way, and with whatever quality of life, come to be part of a meal?

Most of us are brought up eating meat. Historically, in times and places where food (particularly meat) was less readily available, meat signified celebration. Through its rarity, meat brought with it a certain hush, reverence, respect. Its availability was cause for merriment (spear, fire, gather, heat, pull, eat, live), or the slaughter of a single animal on the farm was an occasion (gun, skin, cut, portion, freeze, cook, cook, cook), or being able to afford meat was worth commemorating (save, butcher, hand, prep, roast, slow, pray, thank). There's a reason that cultures all over the world have equivalents of barbecue – meat over a fire brings people together, and has for millennia. However, its constant, widespread and often cheap availability is new.

Now, many of us hardly think about meat. It shows up as a large portion of each meal, and that's that. Perhaps it's considered in terms of iron intake, grams of protein, or as the central pillar of a dish. As my brother once told me, there's poetry in a menu item description, and that rhythm hangs together particularly well when it's easy to point to the central protein component of a dish.

It's easy to ignore an abstraction. When meat is no longer flesh, it's easier to forget.

—

As a teenager I stopped eating meat. With newfound access to the internet, I found myself drawn to and repelled by information about where my food really came from. Like many young people, my sense of injustice was highly attuned. I couldn't stand to know what factory farming looked like and also, still, eat meat. And so I stopped. I remember overhearing my brother and Mum talking in the kitchen, and Mum saying not to worry, I'd get over it. In the meantime, she swapped the meat in each meal for scrambled eggs, TVP (textured vegetable protein), or a veggie burger.

As an adult meat-eater, I look back on my seven years of vegetarianism with some curiosity – I put aside questions about where my food came from, but I don't quite remember how, or why. I remember that first beef skewer. I remember hoping that including meat in my diet might fix all kinds of unease I was feeling at the time. But I forgot all the rest, in a culture that allows – encourages – me to forget. But now remembering has become important to me again, albeit in a slower and more moderate way. These days, I reconsider the size of meat servings, opt for vegetarian meals some of the time, and try to buy higher welfare meat when I can afford to.

I also wonder whether, in my foodish family, my teenage vegetarianism was a form of rebellion. The adolescent version of a baby turning its face away during 'here comes the aeroplane'. Or perhaps, in the small town I grew up in, it was a way of asserting my identity. *I am different. Here's how.* I felt set apart already, and so I drew a chalk outline around my difference. *This. Here. This is my space.* It wasn't only this, of course – my empathy was roused, my disgust joined in. But it was at least partially about my own difference.

—

I'm no exception to the squeamishness around offal, and as something of a daring and thoughtful eater, this fascinates me. Why is it so difficult to get on board when eating offal is so clearly a good idea?

Aside from tongue, I feel ambivalent about offal. I enjoy liver, and ox tail, and pigs' ears. Though I like the idea of that same duplicity in other foods – putting stomach in my stomach, letting brains feed my brain – I wouldn't readily choose some kinds of offal. Tender, juicy, gravy-soaked tongue is a dish I crave, while tripe, on the other hand, with its sponge-like coral, its honeycomb concertina, is something I cannot bring myself to eat. I feel physically revolted by the idea of it moving through my own guts. So I guess I'm halfway on board. In that way, I'm fairly representative of how many people feel about eating offal – getting around the *idea* of it seems to be the stumbling block.

Our objections to offal seem to pivot around the idea of abstraction, in a number of ways.

Meat production is a process so highly abstracted that it's easy to forget we're eating animals at all. Even when language itself doesn't disguise what we're eating ('chicken', 'duck' and 'fish' are honest about the meat's origins, in a way that 'bacon', 'pork', 'beef' and 'seafood' are not), we do a fantastic job of distancing ourselves from the process by which meat ends up in our kitchen and on our plates. The meat of a chicken is still called 'chicken', but it comes cleaned, free of feathers or blood, in a tray with a little absorption packet underneath it. It's a return to that idea of 'duplicity' – the echo of tongue against tongue, stomach in my stomach. While 'duplicity' describes a mirroring or doubling, it can also be used to describe deceitfulness, or lying. In this sense, muscle meats are the real duplicitous cuts – our 'steaks' and 'schnitzels' allow us to forget almost entirely where our food comes from, erasing a whole mooing, clucking, wandering, breathing, eating reality.

Offal, on the other hand, looks so much like itself it breaks the illusion that we're not *really* eating animals: a chicken liver looks like a scaled-down version of our own, an ox heart like that same beating tissue in our chests. In forgetting the bodies of animals, we forget our own bodies too – just as we've been taught to do all our lives.

While the mirroring between offal and our own insides is novel and perhaps a bit sexy in its softness, its blurring of boundaries and its pressing of body parts together, it's also deeply horrific. At its height, it brings cannibalism to mind. The milder horror, however, comes from an undeniable reminder that we are living in bodies of our own.

—

As words leave the mouth, the tongue works hard; tapping and pressing different parts of the palate and teeth to bend sound.

A rush of air punctuated by throat, tongue, teeth or lips: consonants. The tongue works harder for vowels, performing arches and flattenings. There is poetry in the imagery used in speech therapy to allow clients to picture their mouth's mechanisms. 'The butterfly position' describes the way the tongue touches the lower teeth while making 'ee' and sharp 'i' sounds. The tongue moves to produce 'stops', 'fricatives', 'affricates', 'nasals', 'liquids' and 'glides'. The mouth is an instrument we learn to play.

'Tonguing the reed' is what woodwind instrumentalists do to enunciate their instruments' sound. The effect of tongue against reed is similar to that of tongue against teeth or palate in speech.

The strength of our tongues allows us to eat, to swallow; it also allows us to speak. Sometimes we're so good at playing our mouths that the words that fly out of them give us away.

In meditations where I'm asked to identify the site of my anxiety (*Where does it live in your body? What shape is it?*), I often find it tucked under my tongue. (It is uneven and hard like a stone.)

The tongue interrupts. The tongue gets in the way.

The tongue is bitten and saves us.

—

To further abstract our own insides, we tie emotional heft to their existence. The language we use to describe difficult emotions often makes use of those body parts. They become less hidden behind the walls of our outsides, and more expressions of who we are, and the difficult feelings we grapple with. *My broken heart. I hate your guts. I can't stomach him. It's a gut feeling. Gutted. It takes guts. I've had a gutful.* Presented with a plate of offal, we are being asked to eat ugly emotion and difficult states of mind.

The reasons for our objections to offal, then, are narrative. They centre around the stories we tell ourselves about the origin and significance of the foods we eat. It's not that we don't care for offal – it's that we care too much, too deeply.

—

We're socialised to set strict, non-negotiable boundaries around our bodies and their processes. The body as social construct: our bodies exist in the ways they do only because we *live in* them. *Through* them.

In the 1960s, British anthropologist Mary Douglas' work around the idea of bodily boundaries suggested that the work we do to define our bodies in terms of what is and is not part of us is largely arbitrary. Douglas claims that what's 'clean' and 'dirty' isn't determined by anything intrinsic to the object or substance, but is socially agreed upon. Douglas sees practices that define what is 'dirty' and what is 'clean' as a form of social organisation. By classifying and defining these things, communal values and interests are protected. 'Dirt offends against order', she says. 'Eliminating it is not a negative movement, but a positive effort to organise the environment.' She talks about how dirt can be seen as an anomaly within an otherwise 'unified' experience of the world – to define and classify things is comfortable and safe, particularly on a communal level, and uncleanliness threatens that safety.

We go to great lengths to disguise and even combat natural bodily functions, restricting, controlling and hiding the taboo realities of anything our bodies do after the point of consumption – from digestion to death. Simply looking at the organs of the animals we eat, we are reminded of all those things we try to hide. While a steak is nicely butchered into neat geometric slabs, a liver struggles to pretend that it's anything but a liver. Both wonder and horror drive the reaction that follows for many – *I have this inside my body, too*. We become suddenly aware of our own bodies, despite all the hard work we do each day to forget we live in them.

19

I feel like I am Alice (*in Wonderland*), whose story pivots, so often, on food.

Even as she tumbles through the air, falling down the rabbit hole that leads to Wonderland, she manages to grab a jar with a marmalade label on it, though to her dismay it's empty.

All over Wonderland, when her narrative pauses, Alice finds bottles labelled 'Drink me', and cases of food labelled 'Eat me'. Unlike – or maybe *surprisingly* like – the 'eat me' and 'drink me' labels on supermarket shelves everywhere in the Western world, Alice's discoveries don't say how they'll change her life – but they always do. It's unclear exactly how long Alice is in Wonderland, but she never seems to be actively hungry, not until she spies the plate of tarts right before returning home again. Alice's eating compounds the terrible unknowability of her body, but also gives her an option to take control. The sentient foods in Wonderland offer themselves up to Alice, taking on some nonsensical agency in their own ends, and she can only eat and hope, knowing that each time she does this she will get somewhere.

Alice's body becomes unknown to her, and there's horror in this. It's the familiar horror most of us experience during adolescence, and that Alice is running from in the first place when she falls down the rabbit hole, but it's also something more: like the feeling of having slept on your arm, and waking unable to feel your limb. It moves without your will, as if it belongs to someone else.

Without the food, would Alice have been stuck in her strange body in this strange place forever? Here she's forced to act grown up, make difficult decisions, be assertive and experiment to find a body that fits her best. That body tends to change, and Alice needs those changes to make her way back home.

In this universe, food is the centrepiece of worldly navigation. Without it, Alice might have stayed on the pile of sticks at the bottom of the rabbit hole forever, wishing she hadn't let go of that empty jar of marmalade, and without any clue of how to find her way back home. She might have woken in her sister's lap without having dreamt at all.

'Who are you?', the caterpillar wheezes at Alice, waving his hookah around in the air.

She's chasing a rabbit; she's opening a door; she's swimming with mice and birds; she's learning about the oceanic education of mythical animals. Alice can't find her hands; she can't open her mouth without her feet getting in the way. Very quickly, any frame of reference to Alice's *actual* size (whatever that means) disappears.

As she eats and drinks whatever appears in her path, her consumption becomes increasingly desperate. All she wants is for something to change, to feel more herself again, or else find a way back home. Who *is* she?! And how can she ever return – to home, to herself, and to life as she has known it until now?

Jam tarts. Tea. Cakes. Soup. Pepper. It's screaming, soothing, pushing, pulling, always shifting. Everything in Wonderland is either eating, like Alice is, preoccupied with eating and drinking – like the March Hare, whose life is a permanent tea time – or afraid of being eaten, like the many animals Alice comes across who believe she or one of her pets are sure to consume them. Alice can't quite keep track of her own body, and so when the caterpillar asks Alice who she is, she tells him, 'I hardly know'.

Alice hardly knows who she is, but everything around her insists: *Eat me*.

20

The kitchens Dad and I have met in: a home kitchen with laminate floor and burnt patches on the benchtop, and a kitchen with a tiny window above the sink, where we'd wash dishes by hand and watch the dog playing in the yard. A work kitchen with wooden beams holding up the ceiling, and another with wide windows and the sea right outside. At family functions now, my timeout still happens in the kitchen, and that's often where you'll find Dad and me hanging over a bench, talking or at least most comfortable in our silence in that space.

I can picture my growing-up as a montage of kitchens. A flipbook of cooktops that become animated when appraised as a whole. Kitchen, kitchen, kitchen; the memories flash by. We stutter and shudder to life.

In my early years Dad's kitchens were about his absence, but later we met in them, fought in them, laughed in them. Eventually the closed doors opened, and kitchens became shared space.

When I was young, around primary school age, the sound of the pop-out buttons from Dad's chef's jacket dropping into our empty glass fruit bowl meant that Dad had come and gone. I was never awake when he arrived home, and was at school when he left again, so the sound of buttons dropping must have been Mum removing them to wash his splattered jacket.

The kitchen in the seafood restaurant where he worked for many years was (or felt) almost as big as the dining area, which seated a few hundred. The floors in the dining room were stone tile, and the kitchen's non-slip floors were made of glitter. Large windows, the width of the building, opened on to an ocean view. I remember an apprentice sat me in a booth and we ate Freddo Frogs together; I opened the fiddly packets one after another. Dad would have been finishing his shift, or meeting with someone, or drawing up menus by hand. Or maybe he was prepping or cleaning. Whatever he was doing, Dad was not in the booth; he was not there with us, eating Freddo Frogs. He was happy that *someone* was sharing with me, and it was enough to know that I was being included and entertained. I was okay with that too. Curl, the apprentice, kept it up with the frogs. He brought me soft drinks from the bar. I pictured a river under the building made of Fanta, being pumped up through the post-mix gun and into the glass for me. The mere concept of a bar – a bench *just* for making drinks – felt luxurious and excessive. The strange alchemy of the restaurant was another world. Even sound worked differently there: when I laughed, the echo bounced off the cavernous stone walls and tiled floor.

I remember an impromptu, outdoor kitchen: me, about six years old and sitting inside a van on the beach. It wasn't ours – we didn't own a van. Whoever did doesn't have a place in this memory. Dad's workmates cooked meat on a barbecue nearby, and I lay back in his arms. I was unused

to being around so many laughing grown-ups, and particularly unused to being around these kinds of people with
Dad. We watched a storm roll across the bay.

Dad and I worked together for a summer at a motel
when I was an uncomfortable teenager, not yet used to my
own body, or to the incredible highs and lows of my own
personality and its adult emotions. I didn't yet recognise my
capacity for rage, or for empathy to the point of pain, or the
incredible noise I can harness to patch over my introversion
– but it was all there in that summer. Dad cooked food, and
I served and washed glasses. He watched over my fierce
adolescence, so full of wretched feeling.

One night that summer, I reached up into our pantry
after dinner and produced a bag of banana lollies from the
top shelf where snacks were kept. I offered one to Dad as
I sank back into the couch. He looked at me over the top
of his glasses. His eyebrows raised and gaze meeting mine,
this is a look that still makes me wither.

'What did the doctor say?' he asked me.

With the lolly packet in my hands, shame arrived as
a weight at the bottom of my stomach and heat travelling
up my neck. I recalled the family GP's encouragement to
try. My pulse throbbed just below my ears. I got up and
replaced the snacks on the top shelf, and sat down on the
couch again, curling my body into the smallest shape I
could make (a question mark, nose to knees). The responsibility of living in my body, with all its associated fluctuations, was already consuming me then. My decisions, my
decisions, my decisions became real and heavy.

When I was younger, there was a house within a

kitchen (rather than its expected inversion; a kitchen within a house) – Mum and Dad stayed up late at night in the lead-up to Christmas, with every pot, pan, mug and bowl we owned pulled out of the cupboards. They glued slabs of gingerbread together with icing, and all those heavy implements leaned strategically while the sweet mortar set. I wasn't allowed to touch the construction site, but I loved to watch its progress, and to wake to completed houses in the morning, before they were packaged and taken to the local market for sale.

In our last few months at home together, Dad and I checked in over countless instant coffees. In Dad's kitchen now, he offers me a coffee made from his fancy espresso machine. I have to turn him down after the first one, because I can no longer cope with all the caffeine pulsing through my veins. I sit on the bar stools in this other kitchen, in his new life – remarried, moved – and watch him make coffee for himself instead. We talk across the counter as he does.

When I moved out of home I called Dad to tell him about the first saucepan I had bought myself – stainless steel with celebrity chef branding. I later realised it had a metal handle, which was rubbish and resulted almost every time in burnt hands. I didn't tell Dad that bit. I just wanted him in my kitchen for a little while, even though I'd left home and left him behind.

We bridge the gaps with food. There will always be a kitchen for us to meet in.

21

I recoil at my words, now – 'chef' and 'obese'. These are labels that build and damn so much. I feel traitorous for reducing my unsuspecting parents to their abstracted parts – they don't deserve it. They are whole people. I'm co-opting them into my story, using only bits and pieces of them; making a tidy kind of sense where maybe there really isn't any. Their actual lives, like all actual lives, are far more nuanced – and ultimately unknowable to me, because I am not them. (My mouth, my pen, my words – my release of my details on my terms.) What I do know, though, is much less straightforward than these cardboard cut-outs of 'chef' and 'obese'. I know my parents' strength – their passion and resilience. I know they cook for me as a caring gesture, and that when we share meals it's a meaningful meeting place.

The beginning cannot be undone, and this niggles at me. But I also know I need to leave that beginning where it is, because it says so much more about my fear of myself than it does about anything else.

I know that there is more to my parents than these labels, and I also know that attitudes toward and relationships with food – not just mine and my family's, but more widely – are far more mixed than my sketches make them seem. It's tempting to view attitudes towards food as falling at either end of a spectrum, where attitudes which celebrate food lie at one end of the scale – our foodie culture, gourmandism, an appreciation for the finer things in life – and at the other end are those which see food as something dangerous – harbinger of guilt and shame, the insidious moral imperative driving the fitness and wellness industry, and eating disorders both visible and not. We could also think of these two positions – celebration and suspicion – at either end of a see-saw, with our culture constantly balancing between the two (or perhaps sliding back and forth, throwing balance out entirely, feeding this wild teeter-totter action). But I also wonder whether there's actually more crossover between them than there seems at first glance. It's tempting to plonk my parents down on either end of that spectrum, but this isn't where they belong.

My father is a foodie who has heart problems. Inside his arteries are stents; tiny umbrellas which prop them open. More recently, my conversations with Dad often touch upon what he can't eat, because his body rejects it. A hiatus hernia stops him from keeping his dinner down – extreme heartburn hangs him over the toilet bowl many nights. Another little medical miracle saw the top of his stomach tied neatly around his oesophagus, teaching one part of his body to do the job of another. For a little while this helped, but recently the problem has returned. This makes the shared space of eating together more difficult to navigate. We meet for meals earlier. He eats anticipating the discomfort he will later feel.

My mother is 'morbidly obese', and says she feels cornered between two unhappy modes of eating. I recognise this as a feeling I share. She tells me she doesn't feel she can eat 'normally', but is trapped between 'all' and 'nothing'. Describing Mum as 'morbidly obese' puts me on the side of all the world that's worked against her body and taught her to feel so trapped. It feels like a judgement, and I suspect she feels that judgement too. The word 'obese' conjures midsection footage ('the headless fatties') and miserable, isolated lives – whether that's how I intend it or not (and it's not). I wonder, though: if the same were true of my father, would the words feel so loaded? Does the fact that my father is a man automatically mean that food is less of a problem for him? Beyond what 'chef' and 'obese' provide, my parents are other things, too, even solely in the realm of food. My mother is welcome, nurturing. She's *feel-at-home*. She's comfort food and familiar recipes. She's resilient and tender and sometimes small. She's mouth-shut, arms open – she's a soft and encompassing hug. My father is 'go ahead, you deserve it'; bodily damaged but always moving forwards; pushing beyond the body's dispute; rising above it and being stronger. Better. More. Perhaps his years of punishing kitchen work have trained him to rise above his body, and view it as something to overcome. He's providing, always, even now I'm an adult myself.

The desire to apologise is strong, but my desire to acknowledge the confused and grey areas is stronger. It pulls from my chest, my gut, my squishy and lengthy viscera. It comes from my body. If you splayed out all the pieces, you'd find apologies hidden in and between every part.

I live in and through my body, I remember with my body. Some days I am ashamed of it, but ultimately I am resilient and I am soft. I am searching. I write from my body. I notice – with a certain sense of horror – my body, sudden and undeniable. Stretched, folded, hurt and healed. This body is attached to the bodies of my family. Those are the bodies I came from, the bodies that made me possible, the bodies that mine has grown from and alongside. This writing comes from my body (a body of work, a body of words, a body of writing, the body of the text). This writing *is* my body – it lives and breathes, taking on life. It has hands and feet and a beating heart.

—

Sometime mid-winter, a year or two ago, I was on board a tram clanking down a road not far from home. A man I see on my commute every day squinted at me before repeating what he'd just spat across the aisle, but louder. He barked it the second time, 'FAT MOLL'.

Everyone averted their eyes, including me.

It took guts to sit still when I wanted to get off the tram and walk the rest of the way. When I wanted to make myself as small as I could, and cry in the stairwell. Instead, I bit my tongue. Once I'd gotten off the tram, I had a panic attack halfway up the ramp to the platforms at Glenferrie Station. My heart rose to block the bottom of my throat. My lips went numb, my fingers tingled. A passer-by asked if I was okay and I nodded and pushed my face into a corner to wait for my heart to drop back into place. I still see this man on the tram most days.

A word I have learned along the way is 'shame'.

On *The Biggest Loser*, each season started with contestants stripped down to uncomfortable and revealing shorts or sports bras in front of all the people they loved. Through their humiliation, tears, and shame, they'd announce, 'My name is ____, and I weigh _____'. For the longest time, this seemed like a reasonable way to 'help' people; by publicly shaming them.

Dr Brené Brown, whose research and popular psychology books focus on shame, says, 'Shame cannot survive being spoken … It cannot survive empathy'.

These words and this writing live in my mouth. Let me open my mouth wide and show its contents. Despite table manners, and despite knowing better. Let me spit out the words, and ask and ask.

22

'Australians are getting fatter', says doctor and writer Karen Hitchcock in her essay 'Fat City'. Hitchcock argues that obesity is a matter of individual responsibility. As a doctor, Hitchcock wishes patients would stop seeing obesity as a problem for doctors to remedy. While recognising the 'bio-psycho-social factors' that contribute to obesity, Hitchcock also points to personal, emotionally driven sources of problematic behaviour around overeating and weight.

Hitchcock describes one of the cultural roles of food as a potential 'form of entertainment'. By this she doesn't mean our preoccupation with eating, in the sense that we're entertained by our shared meal pictures on social media, or our amusement over theatrical cookery shows. She means the act of eating itself, and how immersive that experience can be. Eating itself is a pastime. Looking to the media and messages we consume daily, it's easy to see how food-as-entertainment has come to be. Food *is* a fun pastime – as the protagonist on many and varied cooking and travel TV programs; as the object of our Instagram posts; or as the executor of theatrics in a restaurant meal. It *is* entertaining.

There is a line there somewhere, though, where this

becomes no longer acceptable. Its exact location, both in Hitchcock's reckoning and more generally, is unclear, but we are made very aware when it is crossed.

Hitchcock also suggests that our emotional ties to food can be incredibly strong, stating that 'most people do not overeat because of hunger emanating from the stomach; they are giving in to a desire to consume – they are seeking pleasure or relief, or hoping to fill a void'. To open her story, Hitchcock describes an obese friend, Emily, whose behaviours around food are mirrored by her modes of emotional expression, where nourishment is a form of kindness both to herself and her loved ones. 'I loved Emily', says Hitchcock. 'She cared for me the same way she ate: enthusiastically, generously, without restraint.'

There's some nuance to Hitchcock's argument – she's pulling out her friend's personal, caring values, and suggesting that perhaps Emily's attitudes to food aren't about physical hunger. At its roots, though, Hitchcock's language is loaded. 'Giving in to a desire to consume' implies that the strong and worthy are able to resist this desire, and those who 'give in' are weak, and should be ashamed of themselves. It implies that the morally superior don't 'give in' – that there's something righteous about resistance. By extension, the 'overweight' body is a marker of weakness or unworthiness. It indicates that its owner is bad.

—

In the young adult TV show *My Mad Fat Diary*, fat and binge-eating teen Rae Earl self-harms, fights with her family, and constantly puts herself down. In Rae Earl I see myself reflected (although I'm twenty-eight when I first watch the show, and Rae's character stands at the bridge between adolescence and adulthood) in ways I haven't in other media.

In one episode, Rae hides in her school library to snack. She's aware that she won't be seen there by anyone who will judge her; the library offers a kind of on-campus haven. Hands beneath the table to unwrap a chocolate bar, Rae looks around to see if anyone's watching. Busted by popular girl Stacey, Rae visibly shrinks, but tries to explain.

'I just can't eat in front of people', she begins. '[I]f I eat unhealthy food then people will think, "Mmm, look at that fat cow, no wonder she got to that size". And if I eat healthy food, then they think, "Who are you trying to kid, love? You didn't get to that size by eating salads".'

Sometimes I have trouble eating in public, too.

She continues, 'They might not say it, but they'll think it. Trust me. I can see it behind their eyes. You know, I used to think that I loved food. But I don't. I fuckin' hate it'.

Rae is a victim of the pervasive idea that large bodies mean weakness and failure. No matter what Rae eats, because she's living in an 'overweight' body, her meals are automatically judged as failures. The categorisation of foods as 'good' or 'bad', 'clean' or 'dirty', 'healthy' or 'unhealthy' seems useful, until the assumption underlying it is considered more closely.

Like Rae, I've internalised an indiscriminate kind of guilt around eating. I've lost the ability to judge what's reasonable, because trying to internalise the cultural barometer for what's okay has tinkered too much with the settings of my own measuring equipment. I feel the need to hide my eating, because I assume that it is *always* inappropriate, unless I'm explicitly being told otherwise. The internal compass that guides this everyday action is no longer readable; no longer a useful indicator of direction. If I'm out with friends and I am hungry, but the people I'm with don't feel like eating, then I won't eat. If I crave something from hunger (as opposed to craving from a place of emotional need or consuming because of panic), I still feel like I shouldn't fulfil the craving – and especially not in public. While working in an office filled with performatively health-conscious co-workers, I opt to eat conservatively – I eat small things, I eat safe things, I eat only what I feel will be judged favourably (as moral, restrained and appropriate) – or else I skip the meal altogether. I skipped a fundraising morning tea at work because I didn't want my colleagues to see me enjoying food and think badly of me. My anxiety whispered, *If you eat that cupcake you are a failure. They will know how awful you are.*

That anxiety does not exist in a vacuum.

You are what you eat. If foods fall into categories of 'good' and 'bad', then *you* are good or bad for consuming them. You are to be watched and considered and spoken about. You are what you are *seen* to be eating. It's not just the chaos of post-binge trash and guilt that piles up against you, but the smaller decisions in your life that make this judgement apparent.

It's the little choices, and the insidious language we use around them – a stow-away in your psyche – until you hardly even notice any more that your meals are morally weighted.

Guilty pleasure. Indulgent. Naughty foods. Sinfully rich. Treat yourself. Dirty burgers.

You're consuming not just food but the cultural belief in the symbolic and moral properties of that food. Even if you don't know you think this, it's conveyed in your language. The criticism of what's on your plate, in your stomach, what makes up your body, exists in other people's looks, your own guilt around food, and the language of 'treats', even (and especially) when it's a little cheeky.

If you *are* a sinner, how do you start to atone for that sin? Punishment is required. Shame, and guilt, and abstinence. Self-flagellation: mea culpa.

And it must be public.

—

I doubt that Karen Hitchcock's friend Emily is bad. I don't feel like any of the overweight people I've met are bad either, for any reason to do with the size of their bodies. There are awful overweight people in the world because there are awful people in the world, period. I cannot see the dotted line that leads from overeating to moral judgement – I mean, I can see it, because Hitchcock's language is just a symptom of the common act of moralising what we eat. The shame she puts on 'obese' people isn't new. But I don't see that as anything but arbitrary, bent toward a culturally endorsed aesthetic. I can't objectively view it as sensible.

And yet, and yet. For a long long time, and still on bad

days, I feel like I've let myself or the world down by being 'overweight'. I feel like I've done wrong by myself, because I feel like I've done wrong by the whole larger context of my place in the world. I can see that the complications in my family's stories in relation to food indicate some kind of brokenness. Something isn't operating as it should.

How to argue with the overwhelming rhetoric of personal shortcomings and weight gain? I am fat and I have failed.

23

Three people I know have died in the past three weeks. Some of them are close to me, and some are not. A member of Danny's family after a protracted illness; the father of a boy I grew up with; and the neighbour whose kitchen window looks straight on to ours. After years of his grumpily ignoring me while I cooked, performing unintentional mirror movements in his own kitchen, suddenly the apartment is empty. I keep wondering if he died in the apartment, and whether they wheeled away his body at some time of the day when I missed it, and whether all this would affect the sale price of the house. The effect of these deaths so close to one another is cumulative; compounded grief. I explain to Dad that I feel spent by, because of, it. I know that it's the way of things, but I want it to stop. Things have been a bit shit lately.

'So what do we do? Eat ourselves silly?'

This is a thing he likes to say: 'Eat yourself silly', as though at a certain point the excess might just flip your sensibility.

I smile and say yes, because it's what I want, more than anything. The distraction of catching up over a steaming, fragrant bowl of noodles. Dampening feelings, which seem to live in my organs, by pouring warm food on top of them. I want that comfort to radiate from my insides.

24

I have been mapping my memories here. I have been trying to use my curiosity as a setting agent, giving memory's movement a solid structure.

Philosopher and academic Edward S Casey acknowledges the 'gappiness' of memory, and builds a language for it. He uses words like 'texture', 'pastiche' and 'density' to describe the ways memory works. He also stresses the slippage at play in remembering, describing ideas of 'clustering', 'compressing', 'distending' and second-hand remembering. Casey's description of memory is visceral and affective; the language he uses gives a feeling of movement and uncontrollability.

In Salvador Dalí's painting *The Persistence of Memory*, watches and clocks melt over a desolate landscape. A hard edge; a tree branch; an organic shape that suggests a face. Dalí came before Casey, but they're saying the same thing: time, memory, narrative, is floppy.

I'm not alone in my attempt to pin memory and the self down for interrogation.

The artist Grayson Perry creates literal 'mind maps' – etchings and tapestry topographies of his innermost psychology. These maps are physically quite large; the footprint of a four-seater dining room table at least. They map

imagined neighbourhoods and locales that depict and justify Perry's personality. This kind of honest self-reflection is
what American writer William H Gass described as 'having
the courage to share the reasons for the catastrophe of your
character with the world'. Perry is entirely accounted for,
catastrophe and all – even if some parts are embellished
and others reduced. In this way Perry's self-representation
resembles the ways we all view ourselves – selectively, and
not to scale. Highly detailed and hand-drawn, Perry's
images look like medieval maps. Here's a marker for a
castle, and here for a forest. Some of these maps have row
houses and laneways, others have hills and guard towers.
Map of an Englishman features a small dark patch at its
centre, labelled 'Consciousness', but the map sprawls far
beyond it, even showing an island surrounded entirely by
seas. One of the waters is labelled 'Agoraphobia'. Another,
'Psychosis'. The land mass is broken up into smaller states
with names like 'Bloke', 'Posh', 'Bitch', and 'Wishes'. 'Fear'
is full of trees and mountains. 'Myth' is entirely made of
buildings (with their own labels including 'God', 'Agnos-
tic' and 'Conspiracy theory'). It's charming to picture the
psyche sprawled out and readable like this. Navigating
someone's personality becomes possible with such directions: what a fabulous resource to provide to new acquaint-
ances. *Head toward Myth; if you reach the trees you've gone
too far.* I suppose this was once the appeal of phrenology,
where the skull's lumps and bumps were thought to indicate personality traits. These kinds of maps themselves
might, however, deserve their own building in that over-
developed neighbourhood of 'Myth'.

I wonder what my own mapped mind might look like if I laid it all out as Perry has done. I feel like there might be a dark section labelled 'Hunger', with subsections 'Appetite', 'Nurture', 'Binge', 'Refuse', and 'Shame'. Perhaps this part lies just over the Date Line, though – like viewing the map of the world and seeing part of it in darkness. In just a few hours, it'll be daytime there, just like the other parts. Every so often it dips into blackness, and then back out. But this map is so much bigger than that neighbourhood alone.

While phrenology and personality maps like Perry's aren't practically useful or scientifically respected, our brains are increasingly being labelled and explained, even mapped, in great detail. It's more possible than ever before to dissect a brain according to each of its constituent parts' functions; it's becoming less like anatomy and more like machinery. Medical imaging technology can now create an *actual* map of the brain, indicating regions that light up when the body comes in contact with the world. That is, as part of lived experience.

It's a dazzling show, all that brain activity. 'Thinking' is too broad. More specific words are useful: deciding, feeling, empathising, calculating, creating. The less abstract ones: smelling, seeing, touching. Those I'm most interested in: Craving. Remembering.

While brain imaging technology has improved in leaps and bounds, there's still an incredible amount that's unknown.

The idea of memory as some kind of mental filing cabinet has been disproven – our memories don't exist in a vault we can flick through and pull out at will. Remembering isn't as free an action as we might like to think; rather, there's an awful lot of involuntariness about it. But the 'filing cabinet' analogy might still be useful when describing sense memory, particularly in understanding how smell contributes to creating memory – and sense memory is one that's particularly tied to how we live in the world.

We taste through smell – 'retronasally' (in that passage where the mouth and nose are connected) creating flavour by breathing the smell of a food. Bee Wilson describes the human brain's ability to interpret and discern between very specific individual smells, saying that 'Each and every time you taste or smell something, the relevant glomerulus [which is part of the brain's olfactory bulb] will take a snapshot of it. These snapshots show up in the brain as patterns, like a map'. Perhaps there's more to the map idea after all.

This ability of the brain to 'snapshot' smells is essential to how we eat, and how we remember food experiences. These snapshots see smells (and by extension, tastes) rendered as 2D 'flat' images. Our strange and squishy brains – relatively small in the context of our whole bodies – can hold 10 000 of these images. These are 'mapped' on to specific locations: this has been shown through imaging brain activity when subjects are presented with various flavour/smell stimulants.

My nose remembers.

Our friends stood at the altar to be married, accompanied by Orthodox rituals – unfamiliar to me, and only newly familiar to the groom. Bells were rung, crowns were placed on their heads, ribbons were tied. They walked in circles around the priest. An unseen choir called in echo from behind a partition. Everyone in the church stood and sat over and over, the ceremony something of an elaborately costumed work-out. As a mark of respect, it was touching – the bodies of nearly everyone in that church (barring the elderly or disabled) were given over to the required movements of the ritual. On the way through the door a sprig of rosemary was pinned to our dresses and lapels. The memory of this wedding, of this standing and sitting, and bells and ribbons, is infused with the smell of rosemary.

'We should save it to use for the roast on the weekend', my partner joked. We didn't, because it was sacred, and not the same kind of sacred as a Sunday roast.

More recently, an old friend died. He was someone who always believed in my thinking and my reading, who gave me challenging books, and talked to me about what he was studying as though I might begin to understand it (Postmodernity, and I didn't, at the time, not at all). I grew up and we saw one another less often as each of his boys moved out of home. Then only at birthdays; only at weddings. At his funeral, we were handed sprigs of rosemary on the way into the venue. It struck me as strange, to have this smell that I'd associated with the ritual of marriage now used to ingrain the memory of saying goodbye. His coffin, the spray of white flowers lying on top. Nick Cave playing and my tears as the coffin was wheeled out the door and into the hearse. The feeling of increasing distance, which neither he nor anyone in that room had agreed to, or were prepared for in any way. And behind it all, the smell of rosemary.

Both of these rosemary sprigs sit in a box of keepsakes we've saved from the weddings and funerals of those we love. The sprigs are together with hard candy, sugared almonds, a cheese board, and booklets full of prayers and hymns and wishes and dreams for the future, and waves and waves and waves of the past. Pictures of people as they were when they were young, and hopes for who they'll be when they are old.

Rosemary is a smell I come across often, and one that warms me somehow. I cook with it: roasted nuts with rosemary, roast lamb and rosemary, roast vegetables and rosemary. It's neither a happy nor a sad smell, now, but the sprigs worked their intended magic: I remember. Rosemary is a smell of hope and sadness, grief and change and new lives, old lives, lives that will never be the same.

By necessity, memory is nuanced and minute – food memories are not just interconnected neighbourhoods, but something much finer and tinier than that: they are individual family portraits on individual dressers in individual houses in individual streets in those neighbourhoods. Food memories are neuropsychological and connected to our bodies. Our very *own* bodies, because as Proust said all along, they force us to remember what only we can.

25

At a local cafe recently, I watched an interaction between a harried woman, her notably more relaxed husband, and their young son. The waitress had brought over two coffees.

'A cappuccino and a skinny latte?'

The father gestured for the cappuccino.

'That's girls' milk', the child informed his mother.

'No', said the mother, 'no. It's …'

'It's milk for mums?' the boy suggested.

I didn't hear her explanation from across the buzzing cafe; I don't know that she had one.

—

A memory from a smaller body – a much smaller body. I was maybe six years old. There was mustard-coloured carpet stretching from one terracotta brick wall to another, and the air was stale. Rows of chairs, also covered in scratchy carpet, faced a board with numbers written on it, and there was a room full of people, mainly women. I knew a lot of them as my friends' mums. This was a multi-purpose community room, and in our little town it housed a great many different activities. It's the same place I later saw a woman tell stories accompanied by her thumb piano, and where I rehearsed plays, and where we attended community group meetings.

My memory of Mum's Weight Watchers meetings is hazy, but it's tied up with that space. The meetings might have happened in other buildings at other times, but this is the one I remember. This space was one where food was set aside as something special, but entirely differently from how Dad did this at the restaurant. I don't remember the atmosphere as negative, but I do remember Mum feeling anxious. I remember a feeling of camaraderie. It was about a shared resistance, and supporting one another in the fight to defeat a common enemy. That enemy was food, the numbers, the scales, the body. Rather, the enemy *is* – people, often women, are still meeting all over the world in similar groups to declare war on these things, and to celebrate one another's victories in the battle.

It looks a little different now – these days, Weight Watchers has rebranded as 'WW'. Its marketing has become more insidious, working hard to associate those Ws with the buzzword 'wellness' and distance the brand from 'diets', which have gone out of favour. The WW target market is terrifyingly broad. Soon after the rebrand, the company offered six-week memberships free to 13–17 year olds, and the company's Kurbo health app is designed for children to track their food intake and set goals like 'weight loss', clocking up 'streaks' for using the app repeatedly. It's similar to the way other social media platforms reward repeated use, developing a relationship with the user that feels very much as if it both exploits need, and punishes it.

—

There's significant evidence to suggest that obsessing about food begets more obsession – that is, the more you focus on food, the harder it becomes to stop. Toward the end of the Second World War, physiologist Ancel Keys ran a study called the Minnesota Starvation Experiment. Faced with a world plagued by mass food shortages, Keys hoped to provide insight into the psychological and physiological effects of 'semistarvation', and find the best methods of 'refeeding' when the shortages eventually stopped. Thirty-six healthy conscientious objectors were recruited and took part in Keys' experiment, throughout which they were all placed on rations similar to the amount starving people in war-torn Europe ate, and each subsequently lost around 25 per cent of their body weight.

The 'semistarvation' calorie allowance as part of the Minnesota Experiment was slightly more than the number of calories commonly accepted as necessary for weight loss as part of most diets now.

Many of the subjects became obsessive about food during the experiment – some collected cookbooks; others mixed their meals with water or let their food dissolve slowly in their mouths to make it last longer. Some fed other people to live vicariously through their pleasure without 'breaking' diet. After the refeeding phase, some men ate excessively – one to the point of requiring hospitalisation. Subjects reported feeling this changed and strange relationship to food as far as two years post-experiment. Physiologically, it took as long as forty-six weeks for the subjects' bodies to return to a state similar to that before their food conditions were changed.

Some of the food obsessiveness that many participants developed might partly be due to the body's response to deprivation, and partly a response to an environment in which food is the central aspect. Our bodies don't recognise *why* we're starving. They don't understand the difference between life-threatening wartime food shortages and an attempt to uncover the 'bikini body' we believe to be hiding inside us, like some matryoshka doll–self to be uncovered.

Why should a body know the difference, and should it care?

—

How does a body speak? How can we even begin to understand what it says, when we're told over and over that it is weak and unreliable? We're told that what it has to say is wrong, that our bodies are duping us, that our bodies are treacherous liars, that they want what we shouldn't have. *Don't trust your body*, we're told. *Your body wants you to be fat, and ugly, and undesirable, and it will betray you.*

And in certain ways the body *does* betray us. Cues that developed over thousands of years aren't useful any more: our bodies misunderstand. We seek out sweetness even though we're eating within a food system oversupplied with sugar. In his immersive memoir *My Year without Meat*, food writer Richard Cornish says that we're hard-wired to seek out umami, and this is part of the reason we have so much trouble abstaining from meat-eating. Our chemical impulses are driving, not our reason (assuming these are, in fact, different things). When meat could only be obtained occasionally, it was fine to eat all that was available – because that wasn't much. The food systems that built our appetites are not the same as the ones we're eating within now.

The brain has its own agenda, and bridges exist between food and brain chemistry, with serotonin acting as an important building block – it controls mood as well as appetite, and both of these have a significant impact on who we are. Decreased serotonin levels have been associated with depression. At its extreme end-point, serotonin is implicated in both mood and eating disorders. At the same time, the region of the brain that controls sense memory also controls emotion. Even flavour comes from here: taste receptors send messages to the brain, which interprets what we're tasting.

The analogy of the body as a machine is used often – if it is to apply, though, that machine would need to be more complex than something with one part for one function. It would need to be intricate and inextricable – pulleys, interconnected cogs, Newton's cradles. Perhaps I'm old-fashioned in my choice of metaphors. Researcher Deborah Lupton suggests that the body-as-machine metaphor has been around for a long time, often changing with the concerns of the day. 'At the time of the industrial revolution, for example, the human body was frequently portrayed as an engine, with pistons and pumps', she argues. Now, however, with the advent of wearable and ever-present bodily tracking technologies (keeping an eye on our heart rate, movement, location, speed, calorie intake, even fertility), we're positioned more as supercomputers or cyborgs with 'networked' bodies. The possibility of exact bodily data offers precision and mastery. The following paragraph of Lupton's reminds me of the hope I long held that strict adherence to calorie counting would guide me out of confusion about my own body:

> From the beginning of discussions of the quantified self concept, therefore, the discourse of trusting data over embodied knowledge, the machine over the human, was evident. Data appeared to offer certainty, while the body's perceptions were represented as untrustworthy, inexact, inaccurately mediated through human experience rather than being objective. In these representations, technology and the data it produces becomes portrayed as offering unique insights into the workings of the human body that individuals' unmediated haptic (physical) sensations cannot. Like other biometric technologies, self-tracking devices are viewed as able to peer inside the body, releasing its secrets (and possibly uncovering its lies).

This view of the body as a machine is compelling; and the connections between brain chemistry and food intake are fascinating. But data is cold and impermeable.

There is so much about the body, too, that is treacherously imprecise. A Fitbit can't peer inside my memory to pull apart a craving, or pinpoint the location of my shame when I'm choosing whether or what to eat in public. The fertility app on my phone can track my mood, but only when it falls into one of four broad categories. Because of all the things the body wants and does without our bidding; because of the stories we tell, and the ones we used to tell and continue to tell even though things have changed; because of the things that can be quantified and understood, and those that cannot; because of our will to be something, someone, different — because of all this, the body remains confounding. It becomes the enemy.

—

Now that I'm older, Mum shares her diets with me more explicitly. Often, they're war stories we trade back and forth. It's a currency that pulls us together in shared combat. We seem to have dug ourselves into this bunker of diet and body talk, and we can't find our way out again.

One of many phone calls with Mum in recent years:

How's the knitting? How's the quilting? How is your dog? What's for dinner?

'I'm thinking of going gluten-free, just to see', Mum says, and her voice swells with hope.

Our weight-loss victories are shared, but they are also often short-lived. All things become possible for our smaller bodies; our perfect lives begin to feel within reach. Just a little more, a little further. A little push. We live through each other's fluctuating bodies: we hold on to each other's changes almost as if they're our own, for better or worse. We fuel one another's hope.

Only 5 per cent of diets work for the general population. This is a conservative estimate; some studies cite figures as low as a 2 per cent success rate for weight-loss diets.

Trials which cite 'successful' diets often count 'long-term' as falling within an 18-month time frame, and don't follow up with participants beyond that point. Most dieters regain the weight they lose, and then some more – the fail rate of diets predicates the existence of the diet industry. Mum and I yoyo in this way together, creating intricate mandalas of punishment and body shame.

When Mum tells me she's giving up grains, I am beginning to doubt diets, and so I offer her little encouragement. The prospect of a new diet brings to mind other failed diets – both hers and mine. They hover in recent memory.

Mine: 12-week Body Transformation, sugar-free, Biggest Loser, Weight Watchers, low-fat, two-week detox, 21-day *Women's Weekly* challenge. The unnamed restrictions: calorie counting, weighing food, portion controls, pantry cleanses, placing napkins over my food, moving bread baskets, making leftovers inedible by pouring liquid or cigarette ash on top of them – so untrustworthy is my hunger. There are innumerable unnamed restrictions for which I have no words.

Soon after Mum's gluten-free announcement, she lets me know she's also given up sugar, dairy and potatoes. I try to picture her plate, and calculate what is now forbidden and what is still allowed. The list seems small.

Six months later, she tells me she's on the CSIRO diet.

'What happened to the grains?'

'It's not interesting any more, I don't think I can keep it up.'

I tell her this is fair enough. I know I wouldn't 'keep it up' either. This brings to mind Hitchcock's idea of eating as a form of entertainment. Perhaps, even when food seems to be in control of us, we're still seeking out what's new and exciting.

I ask Mum if she's still going to weight-loss meetings. She tells me she is, and my worry abates – if there are other people involved in this planning, perhaps it will be kept under control.

The next time I see her, she shares her latest body-related decision.

'I've stopped going to weight-loss meetings', she says. It's winter now, and she doesn't like to drive in the dark.

'I'll try again in summer', she says. And I know that I will too.

—

Once, in hospital during a psychotic episode, Mum had dropped so much of her body weight, I hardly recognised her. She didn't look well; the extent of her longing to be slender had turned her body horrific and shocking. The new smallness of her frame combined with the medicated distance of her gaze made her childlike. When I went to hug her half of my mother was gone. While in an everyday sense our multi-directional (sometimes inverted) caring relationship makes us both simultaneously adults and children, Mum's tiny body on this occasion made this fact plainer than usual.

I had watched her make breakfast for herself a month or two before: a rice cake, just one, with a thin smear of Vegemite across it.

'Mum, surely that's not enough! Aren't you still hungry?'

'Oh, no!' she'd say. She asserted this with such enthusiasm and confidence that I backed down. I don't know whether I believed her, but I did let it go.

I should not have let it go.

It's this loss of control – or, perhaps, this overabundance of control, or the shifting of the seat of control – that makes me hyperaware when Mum mentions new diets.

—

My knee is not working the way a knee should. Muscles are meant to glide with the body; they are supposed to work hard, to tense and flex and stretch: my knee muscles aren't doing any of that. My legs hold me upright, and I walk well, but I wake with pain radiating up and down my leg. My hip muscles and quadriceps aren't doing their job properly. I am not entirely broken, just slightly. Broken in a routine, everyday way.

During a follow-up visit to the physiotherapist, she asks me to lift my leg, pulling a weighted ankle brace towards the ceiling from my seated position on a bench. She asks me where I feel the stretch.

I can feel that my body is doing *something*. My muscles move and flex beneath my skin. But I can't isolate 'where I'm feeling the stretch'; I can't point to or name the pieces of my body involved in this action. It's not just a lack of language, but a lack of understanding my body. The physio suggests some places where I might be feeling the sensation, and I agree with one, but then realise that I've just agreed in order to give an answer, not because I can actually identify the sensation.

I can't hear my body; I can't translate what it's saying. I don't think I speak its language.

26

Brillat-Savarin makes hunger sound magical, almost angelic, and in a way it is:

> ... the human body, that highly complicated machine, would soon be useless if Providence had not placed in it a sentinel which sounds warning the moment its resources are no longer in perfect balance with its needs ... At the same time one's soul concerns itself with things connected with its own needs; memory recalls dishes that have pleased the taste; imagination pretends to see them; there is something dreamlike about the whole process.

Hunger is proof that our brilliant bodies work hard to keep us safe, signalling that we need to eat, but also signalling the need for self-care. Brillat-Savarin's machine seems robust and unbreakable.

However, there exists a different narrative around food, too. There are stories that are warnings against greed. They're cautions against what should come naturally, but often doesn't. They're appeals for restraint. *Watch out for what you put into your body. Beware your appetite. You won't understand why, but these things could get the better of you.*

My hunger makes me hyperaware of food; and this

project, too, makes me see it everywhere. This other food narrative is very easy to see, and it's about what happens if you give space to hunger.

In *Little Women*, a food gift brings about the illness which eventually takes Beth away from the March family – indirectly, of course. On Christmas morning, the girls donate their bread and butter to the Hummel family, who have none of their own and whose children are dying of scarlet fever. The Marches' bread and butter don't stop the Hummel baby from dying. They don't keep Beth from contracting scarlet fever herself. These gifts don't keep either family together.

The nasty children in *Willy Wonka and the Chocolate Factory* are all punished for eating or wanting to eat too much – rolled away, sucked up a pipe, and plummeted down a garbage chute. Charlie Bucket's appetite is modest – even when he's offered more chocolate, he attempts to share it with his family. When he overindulges in Fizzy Lifting Drink, it's Grandpa Joe's curiosity that draws him into the mischief, not his own desire for more. Wonka rewards Charlie's controlled appetite by bestowing his wealth on the boy.

Bridget Jones, sitting on her couch, shovelling ice cream from tub to mouth. Bridget's all body in this moment: arms waving, mouthing along to 'All by Myself', face scrunched, and eating, eating, eating. She's the picture of abjection: a single, lonely woman, unsatisfied in her body and with her lot in life. Aspiring, always, to more.

A bewitched poisoned apple casts Sleeping Beauty into her sleep.

When Hansel and Gretel enter the alluring gingerbread house, they give the resident witch a chance to stick them in the oven. In some versions of the story, Hansel and Gretel are cast out of the family home because their parents can't feed them, and it's scattered breadcrumbs that lead them back home again.

Edmund Pevensie's inability to say no to Turkish delight in the enchanted world of Narnia keeps him under the White Witch's command. Just like the story of Willy Wonka, the Narnia stories are wartime stories. These were times plagued by shortages, particularly of food, and of sugar – exactly the foodstuffs the stories' children were most drawn to.

And perhaps the ultimate: Eve ate the forbidden apple.

27

Eat fruits, eat vegetables, eat conveniently; cook, but don't cook too much. Be all; be nothing. Be slender, be gourmet.

If you're a woman, be delicate in every aspect of your life. Have an appetite, but it mustn't be too large. Take up space, but only a little. Have a sense of humour, but don't be funnier than the men. Smart, but not smarter than the men. Be baffling in your ability to be both. Balance. Be sorry.

During a recent visit to a pub in Horsham, in rural western Victoria, I noticed the menu considerately offered half-serves of the venue's massive parma – an overwhelming serving of food, the size of the dinner plate, and which could only ever be finished by the truly ravenous. They called the half-serves the 'ladies' serve', as though women, by nature, would only ever eat half of a 'normal' sized parma: ladies, your place is with the half-serve. As though, to be a man, you must at least attempt or pretend to want the overwhelming serve. How many men do you think order the ladies' serve when they're less hungry? What do you think the lads say to a man who wants a half-serve? The ladies' serve is a white flag to masculinity. Conversely, to order the full-sized parma, you must have the appetite of a man (because, as in so many aspects of life, the default here is male). This one menu item contains so many demonstrations of the ways appetites are policed.

Of course, I ordered the full serve. Even before the massive heart-shaped chicken–cheese slab landed on the table, I knew I only felt like the half-serve, but I couldn't swallow the menu's language. I say this was 'recent' but in fact, it happened two years ago, and I'm *still* thinking about it. Seething over it. Don't *tell* me what size plate of food a woman should be eating. Don't *tell* me how to be proper.

Perhaps it would be easy to argue that I'm making too much of this. That the menu is just an expression of the ways people eat, and it's catering to its patrons. But this 'add bacon to make your meal extra masculine' attitude, the extension of which dictates men deserve plate-sized serves of protein but women do not, is clearly an expression of the stories we're telling about food and gender.

If the logical argument were worth chasing, we might look to the rhetoric around red meat and masculinity. Burger ads are pitched hard to men, with their man-sized appetites and supposed naturally higher craving for meat. The voice-over is a gravelly male voice talking about juicy all-beef patties. The imagery shows a tower of meat shot from a low angle, elongating the burger's (phallic?) grandeur. But if anyone needs to boost their iron intake, wouldn't it be people who menstruate? Where are the feminist ads that pitch burgers as a responsible and worthwhile act of self-care? Replace the pint of ice cream traditionally associated with pre-menstrual or menstruating women and replace it with a burger. At least that would make sense.

But it's not about logic. It's about the stories we tell about gender and food.

In her article 'Hunger Makes Me', writer Jess Zimmerman looks at the ways hunger is gendered. 'A man's appetite can be hearty', she says, 'but a woman with an appetite – for food, for sex, for simple attention – is always voracious: she always overreaches, because [her hunger] is not supposed to exist'.

Male existence is allowed to be physical in a way that female existence is not. Man-sized things are large and durable. Not just chicken or chocolate milk, but pens, sleeping bags, and sneakers. Men's razors include more blades than women's, as though only men deserve a close shave. Lady-sized things are small. In 2012, Bic released a line of smaller pink pens 'for her'. These differences in size and branding aren't an extension of a natural preference or a reflection of physical size, but a reinforcement of social order. Men's and women's allotment of space in the world differs. Space for their attitudes, space for their noise, space for their bodies. Space for their hunger.

—

My brother's voracious appetite ran wild at those 1990s phenomena, all-you-can-eat buffet restaurants. These were temples of utterly average excess, with bain-maries piled high with over-handled food. A salad bar frequented almost exclusively by mothers; carveries and seafood platters; trays full of garlic or cheese toasts; soup vats; the dessert bar with its soft-serve machine that was always breaking down; and piles and piles of fruit. My brother's plate, stacked with cantaloupe peels, the discarded scraps from his reaching a new 'personal best'. His vomit down the side of the car on the way home.

During my brother's early teens, I once woke midway through the night. In the kitchen spotlights, the unending black of everything beyond it pushing in against the house, he stood cutting rings of onion. The deep-fryer by his side made low blips as the oil rose to temperature. He had whipped up batter from fridge and pantry staples. A midnight snack, but an elaborate one; an intricate form of self-care and self-soothing. A gesture of his self-sufficiency, even as a young man – a boy. When the night is so large, the kitchen becomes a cocoon.

My family's big on midnight snacks. During my own teenage years, I often woke to eat during the night. I did this with my father. If I had done the same thing with my mother, I wonder if it might have meant something different, or at least have been perceived that way.

The divide between want and need for men is often blurred. 'Man-sized appetites' excuse eating habits that in women would attract raised eyebrows or outright questions. 'Growing boys' is a phrase used to explain and excuse (and the need for excusing *anyone*'s appetite is fraught) men and boys' eating in a certain age group; there's no equivalent for young girls' eating, and it's something seen far more rarely. When you *do* see it, it's explained away; patched over with language about guilty pleasures or needing to work out to atone for an appetite which has expanded beyond its usual, acceptable boundaries. When women try to adopt the language of voracity, it's seen as denial, transgression, or failure. Or bravery, which can be worse, because it assumes the gendered paradigm as an unassailable truth, something to be brave in the face of.

—

In his book *In Defense of Food*, author Michael Pollan argues that we've lost touch with the way we eat. We've let scientists and food industries drive what we believe is good for us, rather than letting our bodies dictate what they need. We've stopped listening to our bodies, favouring the noise from experts instead. These 'experts' push what Pollan calls 'nutritionism' – where food is broken down to its component parts, and viewed as no more than the sum of these pieces. This is why we believe vitamin supplements work (new research refutes this), and why foods that contain added nutrients and minerals live in the 'health food' aisle (as though anything outside that aisle is *un*healthy, even though the vegetable section is elsewhere). Pollan points to a pile of flawed assumptions that come out of this premise – that we don't know what is good for our own bodies, that there are 'good' foods and 'bad' ones, and that the whole point of eating is about maintaining bodily health. Pollan calls for a more holistic approach, and one that's far removed from the edicts of nutritionism. He suggests the guiding principles: 'Eat food. Not too much. Mostly plants'. Under this credo, everything we eat is potentially 'health food'.

Pollan's argument lines up with this feeling I've got about what my own body needs, and I've adopted his three-rule value system when I approach most of the foods I buy at the supermarket. I like rules, and by now I know that I'm particularly susceptible to food rules – Pollan's gentle and seemingly sensible (but they all seem sensible, right?) rule seems somewhat safe. What he fails to interrogate at much length, however, is the gendered side of the food marketing and nutrition science industries. While these things appear to exist in the name and pursuit of good health, in practice they tend to target women.

Of course the restraint that women are taught is our place to practise is gendered. This food thing is about my body, but is it also about my *particular* body. What about my body as a woman? And my body as a white woman, a Western woman, a young woman, a cisgendered woman, a small-fat body, an 'able' body. Not all bodies are policed in the same ways. In so, so many aspects I have a lucky body. A body that's overlooked. A body that's been spared so much criticism and questioning.

—

'Consumption' pulls all kinds of things into its orbit.

Foods, shopping and resources. Eating, buying and using.

When buying food in particular ways, consumption becomes mirrored, squared, reflected. A booming food industry pushes the consumption of consumption.

The appetites men are allowed to have for food are, for women, directed towards a different kind of consumption; one that is socially sanctioned. Women are expected to buy clothes and shoes: the safe and approved kind of consumption. But there's also a 'too much' point to *this* kind of consumption. It's okay until it's not okay, and the placement of the line is once again unclear. You hear about women sneaking purchases into the house, telling their partners or housemates that they've had the thing for ages, to avoid being judged for *over*consumption. Because women shouldn't want the things they want. They shouldn't *want* at all ('she always overreaches, because [her hunger] is not supposed to exist'). Everything feels quite normal until one day you're hiding packages and receipts from your significant other to hide the true extent of your shopping. Squashing your desire back into a little box, whose dimensions you weren't aware of until things began spewing out its sides.

——

Each time the calendar returns to January, there's an onslaught of advertising based on the idea of *New Year, new you!* It's all hope and promise on the surface, but some digging uncovers a different story. Doing away with the old you requires new language. Unlearning and reinventing. Why discard an old you, when it's the version of yourself you have the best access to? How much 'you' do you make 'new' before you're no longer 'you'? I remember the Ship of Theseus – a thought experiment that asks one to consider the ship famously sailed by the Greek hero Theseus. If that ship needed repairs, some of it might be replaced – a cannon upgraded, wooden planks changed for newer, sturdier ones. How many replacements would it take before the ship is no longer the one Theseus sailed? Similarly, is this 'new you' still 'you'? At least the old you is one you're familiar with. It's the one loved by your family, your friends. It's the only you there can be. Don't silence her, fold her up, or discard her just because we're on a new calendar page. Don't deny her language or stop trying to listen with compassion to her.

A body's language might be known through its rhythms and sighs. Those processes that happen, near-magically, without volition: hunger, digestion, secretion, regulation. The ways my body repeats its processes as often as it needs to, sloughing off unwanted skin, dropping unused eggs, pushing foreign matter out and away. My flaky body, my bleeding body, my cramping body, my crying body. My sore body. My betraying body. A body will do these things even when we don't want it to; it will give you away without notice. My body sobs and screams and stomps; it will make itself heard. For the longest time, I saw the noise as my own failure to ignore it.

—

The options for writing the fat body are limited. There's an increasing acceptance of bodily functions and their strangeness and hilarity, and these make for both good writing and good reading: they're the stuff of confessional Twitter threads, and clickbait articles that go viral, and even of more serious personal essays. 'I got diarrhea that ruined a date', or 'A sex toy got stuck inside of me'. It's entertaining to read about someone else's body doing something strange and potentially embarrassing. You're not alone in the world.

But for the fat body, there's a context shift. Fat bodies

already exist in dominant narratives as comedic material. Thin actors crawl inside fat suits for comedy (Fat Monica in *Friends*, the Nutty Professor's whole family, Mike Myers as Fat Bastard) or to juxtapose a perfect thin life with a miserable fat one – Netflix's controversial series *Insatiable* became the object of a boycott due to its portrayal of a young adult who becomes thin to exact revenge on her bullies.

The context shift is particularly true for the female fat body. Even when fat characters are portrayed more sympathetically, they're still sidekicks. I want a spin-off *Gilmore Girls* series dedicated to Sookie's life.

Playing into these tropes isn't useful. I want to write about being a fat body (not being *in* a fat body – as Lindy West points out in her memoir *Shrill*, there's not a skinny person in there just waiting to get out), but the acceptable way to do that isn't what I want for myself, or for the bodies of people I love. No body deserves for the starting line to be ridicule, sexlessness, moral judgement, or disgust.

I don't want to make my body funny, I want to make it human. In a world where my body and those of so many people are seen as transgressive, I want not to be alone. To open up, speak up, speak out. I want to be fully, finally, embodied.

—

Be frugal, be adventurous. Make difficult dishes, and make them without effort. Have an appetite, but don't get fat. Want, but don't actually *want*. Don't let your greed in. Don't let anyone *see* the wanting, unless it's the right kind of wanting. Be seen not-eating. Discuss your not-eating choices loudly and proudly.

Also:

Pig out. Treat yourself – you deserve it. Create a wall around your appetites using very specific bricks. We'll let you know where to put the door, how often it should be opened, what should move through that door (for the most part, it's very Willy Wonka: 'Nobody ever goes in, and nobody ever comes out'). Don't go off-plan. For the love of god, don't go without a wall entirely.

These are the rules we're meant to internalise.

How am I to strike this balance? How is *anyone*? I find myself polarised. I have two options: my whole self in or my whole self out. There is no half-measure. As a result, I feel like I'm never acceptably anything. Knowing what I would like to be – positioning the goal posts – is just as difficult, if not harder, than becoming that thing. Do I want to be proficient in the kitchen? Do I want to be seen eating 'properly' in public? Do I want to be thin? The messages we receive around diet and what's 'good' for us are often opposed, and it's confusing.

On the one hand, we're told that we are not our bodies. Or, rather, that we *must* not be our bodies, because a woman's body is the source of emotion and softness. Instead, women are encouraged to strive for rationality, to think rather than feel, and for privileged women, often to become knowledge workers. Women are socialised to work hard at denying our bodies. To deny the existence of the body is to deprive it of what it needs, by withholding pleasure (of food, of softness, of kindness), as well as forgetting what the body does. We're taught to hide our bodies' undesirable functions, pretending they are something other, less capable bodies are prone to. That is to say, *you* are never the person who farted, burped, or became sweaty. You are not the person who had their body betray them. Social horror over bodily functions is so strong that we can turn it inwards, viewing our own body's betrayals as abject. We become strangers to ourselves, padding our self-knowledge with distance. While embarrassments are feared, hunger is perhaps a more casual betrayal. An everyday giveaway that you are human.

On the other hand, we're taught that our worth lies in our bodies, to the extent that we are *only* our bodies. The able body, the beautiful body, the body that measures up to the impossibly high standards set by the media. The body acts as a mirror for social values, and through the complete control of the body we're able to elevate ourselves.

These two ideas might seem dissonant; as though they're opposites. But they're both pointed toward the same thing. *Stop listening to your body*. You have been given your instructions, and that's all that you need.

28

When we know something deeply and intuitively, we're said to feel it in our guts. Some days I wish I could rip my stomach out.

The gut as a whole is becoming the focus of increasing amounts of scientific attention, so much so that it is being given credit as the 'second brain', and the connection between the brain and the gut is being more seriously considered.

Eighty per cent of the serotonin in our bodies exists in our gut. There is also about a kilo and a half's worth of bacteria living in and on each person's body, a large portion of which live in the gut. The guts' residents are colonies, communities: keeping a body alive in the world is a team effort. What gets fed to those bacteria can lead to a boost in mood and general feelings of wellbeing. Giulia Enders, author of the immensely popular *Gut: The inside story of our body's most under-rated organ*, suggests that gut health can affect mental health, with imbalanced gut bacteria a factor in mental ill-health.

Enders also describes the human body's development as comprising three 'tubes'. One for the cardiovascular system, including the heart. One for the nervous system, including the brain. And one for the intestinal tube – 'the gut'. These three 'tubes' develop alongside one another.

I picture the human body as formed along a wire; a braided clump of nerves and pulses and beating, throbbing, wanting. The brain is at one end, and the gut is at the other. The heart sits between the two. They communicate like a tin-can phone, rattling all that noise up along the line.

—

My phone rings. It's Mum.

'I've been looking into gastric bypass surgery.'

I've heard of this. Some fat activists call it 'stomach amputation'. This would remove part of the stomach, giving Mum's body less ability to take in food, and less ability to process it. Her body war is made plain here: she has decided to cut out the turncoat organ inside of her that's sabotaging her goals.

Possibly-slender-mother makes her appearance. Hopeful-mother. Energised and looking forward. Ready for her life to begin for real after the weight is gone. I feel happy for her hope, but I worry whether she understands what the surgery would mean for her quality of life.

'I know, eating is social', she says when I ask her about this. I accept what she wants to do, but not before I spend a lot of time and energy trying to talk her out of it. But this is the deal – if I support freedom for all bodies, then I need to support the freedom and choices she makes for her body, too. I'm just sad that she wants to do it, that she feels there is no other way.

I try to imagine Mum's new, tiny stomach pouch. Half an organ. New and small and powerful.

Research shows that people who have had this irreversible surgery are at an increased risk of suicide or self-harm. Other side effects include lifelong malnutrition (which is commonly 'remedied' with costly vitamin supplements), constant dietary restrictions (no steak, ever again), and something called 'dumping syndrome', which happens when foods move quickly into the small intestine. I learn about the syndrome when I watch a friend shake uncontrollably after drinking a small, skinny hot chocolate.

If the goal is to remove the complications posed by food, I can't see how all these side effects and life changes help.

I picture her as me, in twenty-five years' time, and wonder if I'll still be thinking about this stuff then, whether I'll still be doing battle with my own body, still feeling policed. I wonder if, then, I would support the decision wholeheartedly, and whether I might even want it for myself. I try to imagine willingly placing my body on an operating table and asking to have part of it removed – a part that works well enough, and supports me in living.

These questions are tiring. I can understand why my mother wants to stop asking them.

—

After a positive experience with a young physio who helped me tend to my knee injury – her patience as I figured out what hurt and what helped, and slowly built up and recognised all the ways the body's muscles are connected – I decide to return to the same clinic for a massage. Remedial massage via the physio can be claimed through my health insurance, and that whole system is useless if it's not used, so I make an appointment. I figure that if one staff member at this clinic is very switched-on and provides weight-neutral care, then it's probably a friendly place to go for other things.

I lie facedown on the massage table, topless, with a slender, tanned man standing over me. As he pushes my muscles and moves the pain around my body, he talks from one end of the appointment to the other about what food groups 'we' should be giving up. He tells me, during this 2 pm appointment, that he hasn't eaten yet today, and that he won't until the sun goes down. My stomach flips and my body freezes. I feel unable to get up and leave the room. I lie still and make active listening noises until the end of the session.

By the end of the massage, my body feels full of two kinds of pain. One is muscular, the other is the vague sting of shame, humiliation, anger.

I thank him on my way out. I don't return.

—

Life takes guts. You have to have guts. In my safe and sheltered, risk-averse and mouth-closed existence, I don't call on my own guts very often.

And we humans do have guts – on the whole, we have more guts than we care to recognise. Our actual gut takes up a greater surface area than our skin. Together, the large and small intestines stretched out measure around 7.5 metres in length. As Enders notes, the small intestine folds over and over on itself, compacting into the space of the abdominal cavity. The walls of the small intestine are covered in 'villi' – under a microscope, villi look like fingers. Looking even closer, those microscopic fingers are covered in their own tiny fingers – all reaching out together. They help increase the surface area of the gut. Enders describes how we 'enlarge ourselves as much as possible in order to reduce anything from outside to the smallest size we can, until it is so tiny that our bodies can absorb it and it eventually becomes a part of us'. We don't see this magic because it's locked away inside.

But that's the literal guts. The metaphorical guts are those we aspire to have. I think they're there, too, whether we realise it or not.

My family has been brave; I know we have. I can't always remember specific instances, though. We have been brave when our bodies failed, when our minds failed. When our family unit failed: we held one another aloft as best we could. Mostly, the concept of 'bravery' within our family is linked somehow to stoicism – we keep calm and we carry on. Though what if 'bravery' also looks remarkably like falling apart, but surviving? Embracing collapse, and living through it and knowing that there is an end to it – an 'other side' that we will eventually reach?

The guts we wish to have, and the guts we do not.

I'm learning to rely on my gut as the home of my intuition; slowly, to trust my body.

29

The hospital Mum went to when she still lived on the island was the closest with a psychiatric ward, but it was still a few hours' drive from our home. I was sometimes thankful that it was removed from her day-to-day life. I was glad she didn't have to drive past it every day and remember, or feel the frustration of not remembering through the empty, dark hole left by treatment.

The second-last time I went to see her in that hospital I think I went to comfort myself more than her. I hoped I'd see her and she'd be improved. I hoped that seeing me might repair something of the fracture in her mind, but instead I was met by someone less like Mum than I'd hoped. In between episodes I so easily forget.

Mum's support network at that time was limited to me and her partner, who – for whatever reason – didn't visit often.

When I packed my bag for the train ride, I put in books and a notebook intending to work on the way there – not accounting for my actual anxiety and inner turmoil. I put in a small box of chocolates, imagining that they might bring her comfort. I wanted to pretend that my sick mum was like any other sick mum, and that a simple, caring gesture like bringing in a magazine or chocolates would help – even though I knew this wasn't true. Four little Guylian seashells nestled in golden packaging, made more precious by their size – just four. Maybe I could leave the chocolates there with her and she could eat them and know I was thinking of her, even though I couldn't stay for more than an hour or two before catching the train back to the city.

She shuffled out into the shared lounge of the high-dependency unit, and sat with me in the over-sized, over-stuffed chairs.

First we said nothing.

'Will you be there', her voice pushing through a fog to reach me, 'when the end comes?'

She put her hand on my arm and looked at my face – not into my eyes; the look didn't travel that far. She seemed to regard me instead as a two-dimensional object. She raised her hand and reached past me, grabbing for something. I smoothed down my hair, but she grabbed again and I understood she was aiming for something I couldn't see.

'I got your messages. The beetles.' She uttered the words as though in confidence, so I nodded but said nothing that would confirm or deny the messages she had received. I hoped that they were nice messages. I hoped the beetles she believed I sent her were beautiful, with shimmering wings that spread wide to hold her tight and whisper comfort as they thrummed against her. I hoped they murmured *You are loved, you are loved, you are loved*. But it seems unlikely.

I knew I couldn't give her the chocolates.

On the train on the way home, I ate them myself. Tears rolled down my cheeks, over my mouth and soaked into my shirt. I looked out the window, sad for not being able to say anything that could connect. I ate another chocolate and felt disgusted with myself.

When someone sat down across the aisle I felt shame in my gut (familiar: the body-getting-bigger shame, the eating-in-secret shame) and thought, 'This isn't working'.

30

The idea of inheritance troubles me. I cannot tell if it works like a patchwork, with small pieces of what came before stitched into my being, or if it's more like a picture that has been copied through tracing paper. Is there any certainty in the process of passing down familial traits? Just how precise is inheritance? Do we take on traits wholesale, or cannibalise bits and pieces of our family, choosing or being forced to become little Frankenstein's monsters that mimic our loved ones? All the known and unknown of them. Sometimes I feel inheritance as directionless; forwards and backwards until time becomes a flattened disc.

I want to know whether who I am is predetermined, and whether I am capable of change. I want to know what part choice plays.

31

By now it will be clear that I have a longstanding relationship with my depression and anxiety. It's not a friend, but it's not an enemy either – there's space for us both. After hundreds of bad days, and hours and hours working with therapists, I feel comfortable asking for help when I recognise that things aren't going well in my brain.

This comfort with asking for help is what leads me to The Bad Doctor. Understanding that my food and body relationship isn't what it should be, and desparately wanting help, I started reaching out.

First to my GP, who is A Good Doctor. I cry in the chair next to his desk. He's a kindly older man with a background in psychiatry. He appraises me, no judgement in his gentle eyes, and the photos of his grandchildren on his shelf look down over the room.

'I'm not doing well; it's been maybe … six weeks?'

He makes a listening noise and taps out notes on his keyboard with two fingers. He takes note of my symptoms and issues as I list them:

I've been crying a lot for no reason, and having panic attacks. My sleep has been interrupted, my brain constantly rattling. My eating feels out of control. I have no patience – the other day on an escalator I wanted to punch an old lady for not getting off fast enough. I feel trapped in a whirlpool of brain stuff with no way out.

He asks me what I want, but I don't know. I just want to feel normal. I want a rest. I'm far enough down the hole that I can't see what my options are, so he takes the time to explain them.

We land on adding a mood stabiliser to my anti-depressants, and some melatonin to help regulate my sleep. I have made contact on my own with a therapist, and he says that's fine – covered in part by my existing mental health care plan. This therapist takes a 'nondiet', 'Health at Every Size (HAES)' approach to her practice. These are newish concepts to me, so I read up and try to think of a future where I have embraced the approach too.

—

The new therapist is gentle and full of quiet hope. Her empathy is written in the soft crinkles around her eyes and the way the edges of her lips move as I speak, to reflect what I'm describing. Her office is full of soft furnishings, pastel rugs, candles and pillows. I tell her the same things I've told my GP. She sees my helplessness and steps into case manager mode. She tells me we're going to build a system that includes a team of people on my side. She suggests I see a psychiatrist, to ensure we're treating the right things with my various medications – she would like a diagnosis. So would I. Language has always helped me make sense of things. This will also help us decide on the best approach in therapy.

She pulls up a list of recommended psychiatrists, gleaned from prior patients' reports.

The following day I start looking the specialists up. Only one, a psychiatrist with consulting rooms in a respected private mental health facility, has any availability within a useful time frame. His fees are high, and covered only nominally by Medicare – though this seems normal for psychiatrists.

—

The morning of my appointment with the psychiatrist (The Bad Doctor), I get a text message from the new therapist. She's in hospital and has to take a break from seeing patients. Apologies – contact X or Y if you need to see someone in the meantime. (After some googling I contact X and apply for an appointment.)

The psychiatrist is tall, and folds himself into a couch across from me with his laptop open on his knees. He slouches – at first this seems to be to put me at ease, but as the session progresses he seems more blasé than anything else.

I have done enough initial mental health appointments that I'm quite good at condensing my history (and my family history). This doesn't mean it's easy, or that I enjoy doing it. I walk back over the same ground. I think of the GP who heard it and then laughed and said, 'Well, good luck!'

I mention to the psychiatrist that my eating feels uncontrollable, my body foreign and distressing, and that I've been doing small self-harming behaviours (pushing bull-dog clips into the tender centres of my palms; hard enough to leave marks but not to bleed), which I'm scared might become something more. I've started regarding the sharp objects in my house a little differently.

He appraises my body for a second or two before asking how much I weigh. I'm familiar enough with HAES and my right to weight-neutral treatment that I skirt the question. He asks what I binge on.

'Well, nobody's bingeing on celery, now are they?' he laughs. 'Do you exercise?'

I try to explain how I feel comfortable enough moving when my mood is okay, but when I'm in a hole – like the one that has led me to his offices – I move much less. Getting out of bed or showering is a challenge, let alone getting out for a walk. It feels a bit chicken-or-egg, but I need to be far enough out of the hole to take care of myself. I know *how*. I get the same health messaging as everyone else in the world.

He goes ahead and throws a number at me, guessing my weight when it becomes obvious I don't feel comfortable giving him this ammunition against me. He starts talking about how 'truncal weight gain' leads to treatment resistance, and that if I want to get better I really need to *commit to a lifestyle change*. In short, I am not trying hard enough. He prescribes me a different antidepressant and a CBT app.

—

Therapist X, as suggested by the one who had to take a break, reminds me of what I imagine an older sister might be like, if I had one. She has fantastic posture and wears sensible shoes and slacks, but she also laughs in a way that makes me feel like we're in cahoots. Her office is likewise filled with soft furnishings and pastel cushions. It smells like bergamot and ylang-ylang. I feel my heart rate slow as soon as I walk in.

After doing the initial intake / case history dance for the third time in two weeks, she tells me about what she feels might help: keeping someone on my team who can monitor the chemical side of things (though probably not The Bad Doctor – she is horrified when I tell her about the last appointment); working with her on what she calls a 'behavioural activation approach' (finding achievable actions that can help me dig myself out of the hole); and borrowing from dialectical behaviour therapy (which doesn't mean much to me at that point). She says we will come to learn my moods intimately so that I can see a depressive episode or a binge coming and intervene early.

This is a concrete set of actions that I can work on, add to my toolkit, and carry with me into the future. I'm ready.

32

I'm not just spilling – I'm not just opening my mouth and letting this all dribble out. This writing is not purely confessional.

Putting aside the loaded language and the implied worrisome femininity of 'confessional' writing, I'm not simply emptying my insides on the page. I am not spilling my guts for you. I'm not just laying it all out for you to turn over. I'm doing some of the extraction and turning over myself, and I hope that I'm spinning and weaving a more sensible kind of textile out of all this detritus. A confession atones for wrongdoings – but I have done nothing wrong.

Have I?

I cannot speak for all the characters in my story; I can only speak for myself. All I can really claim ownership to is my own story, and even then – it's flawed and faltering.

A confession comes from the mouth. It lines the cheeks and tickles the throat. It sits heavy on the tongue (alights upon buds, taste centres, muscles and platform for all the words that get spoken) before moving out into the air – said. Unable to be *un*said.

A confession adds something to the world – travelling on air, it becomes a thing, *out there*. It can't be inhaled back, forced to sit silent and safe in my lungs. It takes up a kind of space, exists in the world. And *this* confession isn't just mine. It's mine, it's ours, it's yours. I've made all this noise. I've moved all this air.

Once it has left my body I am stripped back – vulnerable, fragile, naked. I am pure body, with all eyes on me. I bring this on myself. Please look away.

I don't understand how or when my story shifted – between there and here. I started at food as comfort, food as home, and ended up feeling guilty and confused about it. Are these separate things? Perhaps it didn't shift at all. Perhaps it was just like a lens coming into focus, the blurry things becoming clearer and more articulated. I don't know. I don't know.

I pay attention to my body. I pay attention to the parts of me that remember, and the memories that don't just live in my mind. In reaching for the vertically placed cutlery in a restaurant my hands remember reaching for the spoon, laid horizontally across the top of my childhood plate. In the tang of raspberries hitting the sides of my tongue, I remember my grandparents. In the weight of shame in my gut and in my throat, I remember my father's heart attack. I taste food, and my body becomes a series of hotspots. I'm like the body from *Operation*, lighting up when touched. I'm almost exactly as graceful as that game, too, in my remembering. It's not a reverie like Proust's backward dancing, but more like me jerking and honking my way back into what's been. My body acts, always, as the reminder, with food memories tied here and there; like yellow ribbons to tree branches.

33

One kitchen.

During the final year I lived at home, my teenage body ran on unfathomable fuel and irresponsible amounts of sleep. I went to bed at 12.30 am and rose before 6 am. Somehow, I still woke up halfway through most nights. Dad's newly diagnosed depression had him doing the same; our body clocks were reliably out of whack.

At 3 am, I would walk out to the kitchen. Downlights cast a soft glow on the brown laminex benchtop. Many nights Dad would be there, trackie bottoms and a loose t-shirt hanging off his tired frame, worn moccasins on his feet. He would have a spoon in one hand, another spoon ready to give to me.

He'd open the pantry door and there would be shelves stacked with food. Half-eaten packets of things we'd found shopping in Chinatown and wanted to try, tupperware full of rice and pasta, the top-shelf hiding spot of lollies in tins and packets. The middle shelf was the home of spreads, a wonderful variety of things to put on bread, and this was where Dad aimed at 3 am.

The peanut butter stuck to the roof of my mouth and my tongue, but this was okay; we didn't always talk. We passed the jar between us until we were ready for bed again.

I replaced the jar in the pantry until the next night when we'd meet in the kitchen's half-light.

Comfort food is peanut butter straight from the jar.

Right before I left home, at Christmas time, Dad had his heart attack. Stents helped the blood flow more easily around his body; his heart didn't have to try so hard. Almost ten years later, a quadruple bypass followed another close call.

At the hospital after the bypass, Dad slept with his face scrunched into a pained scowl, like a petulant child. His breathing was regular but shallow. I'd heard before of new parents watching their babies closely as they sleep to make sure they haven't stopped breathing, but that sometimes babies do seem to fall silent in the night, despite being very alive. I watched Dad with the same tension. His chest barely moved. Along his arm ran a fresh scar – I felt the familiar recoil that I often do when I see scars on other people's arms. Most days I feel that the scars on my own arms and legs have been magically absorbed into the landscape of my body, and manage to look past them, but the physicality of other people's pain always comes as a shock I feel in my own body; with my limbs and in my stomach.

The doctors had taken a vein from Dad's arm and used it to build literal 'bypass' options for the blood moving through his heart and encountering blocked arteries. Crack. Bone saw. Within my father's chest was a fresh construction site, with its brand-new complex network of roads, bridges, and detours. Were his insides now shiny like a car after it's been serviced; did it smell like tar; did the doctors need to force his pieces back into place or does everything in the body have its place so clearly demarcated that it just goes back there after it has been removed; do all open chests really look similar enough for a doctor to know what to do inside them?

My father's mortality became suddenly, painfully obvious: one day he will die, and most likely before I do. It was the immediacy: how preventable this scene was. It was the guilt: how often we'd connected over something that had done such damage over a long time. I pictured Dad's artery walls coated with all the peanut butter we'd shared in silence. His insides a sticky, viscous mess.

Guilt showered down on me. The daily reminder of my own body was a personal failing – a moral shortcoming, my inability to keep up with what's good, what's right, what's needed – but my father's body shutting down was something else. It screamed the injustice of existing as a fleshy, limited, imperfect machine. It screamed that a body can decide, at any point, to reject what's being provided. Or a body can become martyr to it, like Dad's had, saying *It's okay, I'm fine, this will do*, but then, one day, just giving up. And that even when we do the best we can, bodies give up all the damn time.

If we think of the body purely as a machine, then perhaps after all these surgeries he's simply upgraded. He jokes, each time he goes in for surgery, about advancing to a newer model. But I can't see a body as a machine if these machines, whose job it is to carry us around, so often fail. There is cruelty, and cost, and heartbreak in its planned obsolescence.

34

I acquire cookbooks in the same way I acquire other books. I collect, collect, collect because I'm struck by an enormous fear of missing out.

Looking at the cookery section of any bookshop, it's clear that what's being sold is never just a book, but actually an idea.

It's like any advertising: in ads for antihistamines, you see a family frolicking through a field. Harmony and ease abounds. In an ad for specialised toothpaste that fights tooth sensitivity, a guy talks about once again being able to eat ice cream with his daughter: he describes the way they look at each other and laugh. Viewers with sensitive teeth and daughters and a yearning for ice cream moments superimpose themselves on the ad, substituting their own lives for the one it depicts, and it feels hopeful. Like all advertising, we're not being sold a product, but a feeling, a lifestyle. An idea of ourselves as better than we currently are. Cookbooks are no different. You're buying the recipes, but also a beautiful kitchen, a dining table surrounded by loved ones, and a life that contains from-scratch meals every night of the week.

I am no exception: cookbooks fill me too with hope. I'm buying inexhaustible willpower, and the energy to prepare a satisfying meal every night, and a spotless kitchen bench. I imagine all the connections that might be made over the foods I see in the pages of my cookbooks, and get a feeling in my gut that heats me with promise.

When I first move out of home, I buy basic cookbooks. They teach me how to make muffin batter, and casseroles, and garlic bread. Soon, I turn to Weight Watchers. Then graduate from Weight Watchers and take up other diets, jumping from hope to hope, until finally I land upon wholefoods, wellness, and clean eating. What lines my shelf favours 'healthy' cookbooks, those that use novel and trendy ingredients. Accordingly, my pantry is soon stocked with chia seeds, brown rice syrup, almond meal, and coconut oil. When I cook with these things I feel the same sense of wonder I felt when Dad and I whipped up marshmallows, or when he handed me the ice cream container full of honeycomb. Cooking with these things is both theatre and alchemy.

Coconut oil sits on a shelf in my kitchen, solid at room temperature in the winter months. I watch that jar like a storm glass: its contents thick and solid when it's cool, but as the weather heats up it becomes less murky, eventually totally clear.

Dad had never heard of coconut oil.

'You mean palm oil? Don't use palm oil. It's so, so bad for you!'

'No, *coconut* oil!'

'You sure?' He seems to think that because he hasn't heard of it, it mustn't exist and I must be confused. I don't realise at the time that while they're not the same thing, they're not so very different, either – that it's just a tricky wellness diet rebrand.

Dad visits for coffee. I give him some of the silky, thick paste to try and he looks at it with badly masked suspicion before bringing it to his mouth. His jaw moves in that slow way it does when he tests for tastiness. (Does this moment measure up? Is it to taste? Does it fit the agreed-upon criteria for those stories that make the menu?) He pouts and nods, finding it to his taste. I have convinced him that coconut oil exists.

Coconut oil melts at a very low heat, making it perfect for caramelising onions. Rather than the uncontrollable almost-burnt onions made by frying with olive oil and water or balsamic vinegar, coconut oil makes onions glossy and soft, massaging them until they relax and are infused with the oil's natural sweetness. Looking over my collection of cookbooks, full of this kind of cooking, I wonder if food could mean something different – less fraught – to me.

For a while, this is my salvation: foods 'as close to their natural state as possible'. I become skilled at deciphering nutritional tables and ingredients lists. I stand near people (mostly women) like myself in the supermarket aisles, identifying the good sugar and the bad, the right fats and the wrong ones, spending too long turning a product over in my hands and assessing all the possible alternatives before committing it to my basket.

For a while I become obsessed with food purity, as though it might absolve something in me. It seems, at first, like extreme foodism. It feels like mindfulness. I spend up big in the health-food aisle, buying packets, jars and boxes of 'clean' foods. I shop at the perimeter of the supermarket. I sign up for wholefoods eating and exercise programs, and they do what they say they will. I avoid processed foods, I become more proficient in the kitchen, and I bask in the saintly glow coming from my insides. I float. Untouchable.

—

Food writer Bee Wilson describes the rise of clean eating as 'a dysfunctional response to a still more dysfunctional food supply: a dream of purity in a toxic world'. In her hugely popular *Guardian* article 'Why we fell for clean eating' (published mid-2017), Wilson pinpoints a shift away from simply eating healthfully and nutritiously, and toward a food movement with moral and class overtones, largely promoted by non-experts with something to sell. It's difficult, says Wilson, to unpack the solid nutritional advice at the centre of the hugely profitable clean eating industry, and extract it from commercial interests, guilt, shame and aesthetic drive. In a similar (May 2016) article for *Vice*, food writer Ruby Tandoh describes how 'The diet books of our parents' generation were all tacky evangelism and shouty miracle claims. But our health is more muddled now – we live in an age of "obesity epidemics", horse-meat scandals, and fears over hidden food nasties and carcinogenic additives. "Wellness" lifts us above this food chaos'.

This is what I yearn for – to not be confused by the difficulty of food and its shifting rules. For a simple alternative that I know to be good. I, like Tandoh and countless others, thought that clean eating and wellness was it. Having not just permission but encouragement to eat an avocado (which many diet plans see as full of fat and therefore to be eliminated) felt powerful and radical. Foods previously off-limits became superfoods, and promised weight loss, satisfaction, energy, and a certain glow. 'There's nothing left to be fearful of when the bad food is labeled "bad food", and when what's left is a miracle cure', says Tandoh. She describes the clean eating movement as 'a precarious path between diet regimes and a love of food'.

In *Wellmania*, author and journalist Brigid Delaney calls attention to the endless optimism (and desperation) of the human spirit, which is the prey of the wellness revolution. She observes, 'We desire to be clean, lean and serene. What is this struggle but trying to overcome death and disease? What is *wellness* but the futile struggle against inevitable loss?'

—

Queensland-based academic Donna Lee Brien suggests that eating disorder memoirs are actually a subset of food writing and food memoir. Both food and eating disorder writing are preoccupied with 'foods and their power; rituals of consumption; taste and a relentless quest for flavour; and the search for self through a relationship to food'. Both connoisseur and disordered eater often understand the finer details and power of food intimately, whether that means how to create a tarte tartin, or how many calories that tarte tartin contains and how long it would take to 'burn off' – or, also likely, both. Control is paramount for both.

I'm in here somewhere, they both say, and their search starts by cataloguing kitchens and consumption. Though disordered eaters and food lovers seem like they might display opposite behaviours (though by now it should be clear they don't), the written genres created by these communities share much. In the same way, wider discussions of and attitudes towards how to eat 'well' share common ground. The stuff that's working and the stuff that's not working can often be the same things. The encouragement of these behaviours seems tied to the body size of the person exhibiting them.

I can't remember all the rules now; there are just too many.

—

With its rules around what's 'dirty' or 'toxic', clean eating and its accompanying 'wellness' is only accessible to relatively few people. It's big business, with cookbooks (of which I have had many) and dietary programs, as well as accessories like fitness gear and food products. The faces of the movement are impossibly flawless and chiselled, young, often female. They're shot in high key, wearing white flowy garments in summer and wrapped with carefully styled woollen blankets in winter. Their kitchens are spacious, their smoothies vibrant. Their Instagram followers are in the tens or hundreds of thousands. All these tokens of wellness and goodness carry a price tag (often a hefty one), as do the high-quality organic and rare foodstuffs that pepper 'clean' menus. It turns out to be very expensive to give things up.

This is the industry through which Belle Gibson, Australian clean-eating blogger, gained her success. Through her *Whole Pantry* app and cookbook, Gibson claimed to be treating and recovering from brain cancer through a wholefood diet and outlandish wellness practices. In 2015, two *Herald Sun* journalists launched an investigation that showed her story to be fabricated.

Gibson's case is echoed all over the world in different ways, and the incredible reach of this industry is reflected through what's available in supermarkets and on cafe menus. Like diets, clean eating and the wellness industry feed on the inexhaustible human potential for hope. As Wilson states, 'clean eating confirms how vulnerable and lost millions of us feel about diet – which really means how lost we feel about our own bodies. We are so unmoored that we will put our faith in any master who promises that we, too, can become pure and good'.

The rhetoric of clean eating is a new, jazzed-up version of a good old-fashioned diet, with overtones of status anxiety in its restriction. It's packaged as a 'lifestyle change', but this mode of eating uses language based on 'cleanliness' and 'purity'. It still draws rules and comparisons around 'good' bodies and 'bad' bodies. There's a right way to do it.

'Orthorexia' is a relatively recent term that describes an obsession with limitations. It's not a medical term just yet, but it is being recognised and making its way into discourse, either as 'atypical anorexia nervosa' (atypical in its issues and drives), or as a kind of disordered eating that interrupts how a person lives. In orthorexia, over-adherence to the rules designed to 'keep us healthy' makes the brain dizzy;

an inability to bend from these rules narrows the orthorex-ic's life to the pursuit of perfection and nothing more. The logic of orthorexia suggests that if some rules around what it means to be healthy – how one should move, what one should eat, what one should *not* eat – are good, then more must surely be better. Wellness becomes a skill to be mastered. And the overabundance of advice within the health (food) industry makes it easy to grab hold of these messages as they pass by. This is excess too, but not one that's often recognised as a problem.

And like any other diet, for me, the restriction of the insistence on wholefoods, and the guilt of even the slight-est movement outside of the rules leads to a binge cycle. I become hyperaware of my body, and hate it with everything I have. To live up to the wellness ideal I cannot let my guard down for even a second. I watch the scales closely. Exhaus-tion wins out.

I fail, I lose, I crumple in disappointment at my body and my brain.

I try again.

—

Nobody else in my family collects cookbooks the way I do. Dad and my brother approach cooking intuitively, and Mum has a collection of things she has always made, and seems always to have known how to make. My brother snacks on sweet things even though his teeth can't take it; Dad cooks in huge batches and has three freezers for the outcomes of those productive jags; Mum always has a different cake, biscuit or slice on offer when I arrive.

We are all hungry for something, and this is my hunger. Insisting on cooking differently – following new instructions, learning new skills – I am kicking against my family with both feet, not for a lack of love for the people themselves but in desperation, to find a new way to relate to one another and connect. I'm about halfway there. On good days I am a wholefoods goddess, making chia puddings and coconut truffles, or braising my way to something both nutritious and rich. I am clean, I am pure. On bad days I feel the fracture again, and wonder whether I will ever be more than the sum of my parts. I binge and forget how promising the new way of cooking and eating can feel.

On those days I know, it's still not working.

35

A few years ago while visiting the USA, my partner and I toured a Louisiana sugar cane plantation. The tour guide explained customs of the late-eighteenth- and nineteenth-century plantations, built on the backs of slave labour, scaffolded by cruelty. The food industry has a long history of breaking bodies. Little bits of trivia detached the plantation stories from their devastating lived realities. For example: when visiting a plantation for business, you'd find a pineapple in your room. It meant, 'Welcome'. A few days later, you'd find a second pineapple, with its top cut off. It meant, 'You have outstayed your welcome. It's time to leave'.

I wonder whether, in writing this, I have chopped the top off my own pineapple. Telling the stories, all these dangerous and unapproved stories, is a purge.

Bee Wilson says that

> When you try to get back to the past through food, so
> often you find you can't, because either the food has
> changed or you have. This is one of the many things
> that makes packaged foods so alluring. With their bright
> labels and never-changing fonts, they seem to offer a
> continuity with the past that you just can't get from

other foods. The easiest way to get the drugstore hit is to keep going back to the drugstore.

Cooking myself into oblivion. Eating myself to connection, and to disconnection. Passing the bread. Blowing out the candles. Sending photos of our dinner as messages of love: *I cannot be with you but here is some salmon I just cooked with a sauce made mostly of butter.* We don't say this, and we don't say, *I'm so sorry and sad that Mum's sick.*

Realising that feeling comfortable in your body isn't something you're born with, but something you fight for.

Proust 'sensed that it was connected to the taste of the tea and the cake, but it went infinitely far beyond it, could not be of the same nature ... It is clear that the truth I am seeking is not in the drink, but in me'.

There's nothing wrong with my body. There's nothing wrong with my body. All bodies are good bodies. But this one, some days ...

Like any purge, eventually there is nothing else to be rid of.

But there is an immense possibility that comes with being empty. There is space to be filled back up. The ambition and hope in deciding what to eat. The tyranny.

36

Comfort is mashed potatoes. Comfort is adding cheese or garlic to the mash – comfort is saying *yes* to both, why not, and creating a mountain of the stodgy fluff, placing a knob of butter into it and pretending it's a volcano when the butter melts and comes trickling out. Comfort is syrupy Dutch waffles microwaved for a few seconds and eaten, oozy, with a warm drink, or placed on top of a steaming cup of coffee to go pliable and tacky. It's next-day boiled rice zapped with butter and brown sugar for an imitation caramel rice pudding. For breakfast. It's fresh white bread stacked with hot chicken and slathered with buttery, whole-egg mayonnaise; or that same bread with strawberries, the fruit's colour spreading like dye into the soft white casing. Sometimes I seek these things out myself – most of them have always been within my reach even when I was young and microwave cooking was all I was allowed to do. Comfort food is often easy, often simple. Sometimes it doesn't matter *what* is being served – the sense of comfort comes from having it served with love or concern, by someone who matters to you. It's not about the food, it's about this proof that there is a safety net. *You will always be there to bring me a bowl.*

As a child, there was also tea, which I didn't like – all black and tannic. Mum drank tea when she felt sick, and so I was told that tea should be a comfort. I'm sure it *can* be that, for some people. But what creates a comfort food is that it's tethered to memory, and to experiences of feeling cared for, safe, content. The only time I drank tea was when I was sick, because Mum did too. All it achieved, really, was to leave me with an unfortunate taste association. When I drink tea now, I feel sick. My tea-drinking friends see this as heresy. Living in Melbourne, good-quality coffee is ubiquitous if expensive, and that comfort is my preference.

Of comfort eating when sick, Ruby Tandoh (in her warm and tender food book *Eat Up!*) suggests that food can be medicine, that 'these foods might not be packed with precisely the vitamins and minerals and macronutrients that your body really needs right then and there, but they will make your soul soar, and sometimes – when the very fabric of your life is one big snotty tissue – that's all you really need'.

Later in life, this ability to soothe with food has shifted from Mum, from Dad, to my adult self. As I have become who I am going to be, I also become able to comfort myself. I recognise the flavours that warm me. I learn the pleasure inherent in braising. I melt with the sweet garlic and softening onion smell that fills the apartment right to its back rooms, crawling through the crack beneath closed doors, and entering closed rooms until I'm surprised by how much they smell like the kitchen. I begin to see simmering as the word 'blip' in my mind, bubbling away until I have something bursting with flavour, despite starting with the humblest ingredients. I learn to translate time into flavour, and flavour into comfort.

197

—

Self-sufficiency relies upon intuition.

Real, skilled cooks don't use recipes, and this is how I aspire to cook, too.

In the kitchen of ethical butcher Tammi Jonas, I watch her whisk and whisk, and when she calls for a little more milk, I know she's confident in what she's doing. She's giving the dish what it needs, in much the same way the dish is giving her body and her deepest self what it needs. Biscuits and gravy with her farm's bacon: this is her comfort food, and she's chosen it for its significance to her. Tammi cooks with her heart.

In the kitchen of my writer and dancer friend Adolfo, I watch him shake a spice jar full of bright yellow turmeric, pinch by pinch, until the bubbling brew on the stove hits exactly the right colour – he cooks by intuition; by smell and colour and the feeling from behind his favourite spatula. He has a special connection to his body's needs already because he's so aware of how it moves. He brings that sensibility to the stove, and his muscle memory for this dish he's made all his life takes over. He struggles to narrate, using language, exactly what he's doing, but his body clearly knows.

These capable home cooks are self-sufficient, not needing a recipe to tell them what to do. They can see what they're doing, what they need, and where to get it sustainably. MFK Fisher recognised that cooking can be an effective way of fulfilling all kinds of hungers, both bodily and not. People who feel connected to their food know how to feel those hungers, how to name them as hungers, and then how to satisfy them – this is where feeling comes in.

The body is capable of harbouring alternative pleasures. A massage can be at once painful and a relief. A long walk to the top of a massive hill can be at once a reward and torture. The enjoyment of food can be more than one thing, too. Food can be a pleasure in itself, but also carries other kinds of joy.

Cooking and eating can be pleasures because they sing of self-sufficiency: the ability to know what's needed and procure it. The ability to provide for oneself. Maybe this is found by growing food, or by going to the supermarket. Maybe it's found by transforming the contents of a 'bare' pantry into something edible: over-ripe bananas into a fragrant, dense banana and thyme cake; or a handful of spring onions trimmed from a balcony pot plant to garnish chewy, crispy Asian pancakes. Maybe it's just knowing which church the soup van will pull up at, and knowing how to ask.

Food can also be a pleasure because of its simplicity, because the pleasure of intuition followed makes the body and the mind – the whole self – a more comfortable place to be. When my body feels like a cauldron of emotion, knowing that I can ascertain what I'm feeling, and also what I need, feels like an achievement. Sometimes it makes me angry to have to re-educate myself like a child – *what do you feel like?* – but this also turns out to be a very challenging question. What *do* I feel like?

These alternative pleasures are about finding enjoyment in *food* still, outside of any preoccupation with body image or nutrition – but they still somehow come back to food as more than food. It is self-sufficiency, simplicity, and intuition also.

—

Watching Nigella Lawson's cooking show *Simply Nigella*, I've noticed that she says 'I want' quite a lot. She says it as she's adding ingredients to a dish; sprinkling things out of jars or shaking canisters.

'I want chilli flakes', she says. 'I want cloves', or 'I want cinnamon'.

In the opening of her book *How to Eat* (a fabulous title, because even when we're asking *what* to eat, what we really want to know is *how*), Lawson writes, 'I have nothing to declare but my greed' – she writes this without apology. You cannot cook well unless you eat well, she warns – and she simply loves to eat. She knows what she wants, and readers are invited along as she seeks it out. Like the strange, sideways reward of viewing peers' breakfasts on Instagram, following Nigella's cravings is oddly compelling. Watching her sneak into the pantry to fulfil a late-night craving gives viewers permission to do the same.

In a chapter introduction in her *Simply Nigella* cookbook, Nigella considers so-called 'comfort eating': 'Rather, *discomfort* eating is what that term always implies to me, with its random, rushed, unassuageable hungers – eating, dislocated from appetite, as a means of self-persecution, holds no comfort for me' – this woman is in control. Her *want*-ing doesn't derail her – it makes her entirely accountable and powerful. She's utterly sexy in the way she knows what she wants, and uses sensual, quietly provocative language to share those desires.

Nigella's ability even to vocalise her desire is a victory – she's a woman in a kitchen. I admire her for so many reasons – she can put her finger on what she wants. She can say what it is. And she can fulfil it. She is entirely self-sufficient.

—

With the help of a very good psychologist who specialises in food and body issues, I am learning new ways. I eat five or six times a day – three meals and two or three snacks. I leave no more than four hours between eating – at first as a matter of routine, and then because it turns out to be how often I need to eat to think clearly and feel satisfied. Mostly, I know what I will be eating next. I eat what I feel like.

I learn to run through options: crispy salty? Sweet soft? Tangy? Sweet salty, even? Do I want something crunchy, or something smooth? Something that melts in my mouth and pools on my tongue, or something coarse that lands more heavily in my stomach? How does my immune system feel – would fruit help? Everything becomes possible and permissible.

These are the new rules, and the only ones, and I only think of them as rules because routine and ritual are what keep me breathing. I let them dovetail with a full life, which is sometimes unplanned. I bring them to family meals – inside of me, but they don't interrupt. Life just feels smoother this way.

I have permission to make any food decision I want. I return to the family table, to the pantry, to my own kitchen, and most days I bring with me less fear and more self-compassion.

Ruby Tandoh calls it 'mindful eating', saying 'it's a way of putting your mind back into your body and just for a moment, letting yourself be'.

In calling for a paradigm shift away from weight-based assumptions about health, HAES champions Lindo (formerly Linda) Bacon and Lucy Aphramor call this bodily self-trust and self-compassion in relation to food 'intuitive eating'. Intuitive eaters, they say, 'increase awareness of their body's response to food and learn how to make food choices that reflect this "body knowledge". Food is valued for nutritional, psychological, sensual, cultural and other reasons'.

Evelyn Tribole and Elyse Resch, whose book *Intuitive Eating* is the bible for this thinking, call it 'a process that honors the validity of one's inner voice'. A chapter added to a newer edition of the book refers to multiple studies that underscore the science of intuitive eating. Not only do studies show that dieting 'predicts increased weight gain', but also that intuitive eating is associated with better physical and mental health outcomes, regardless of body size.

One of Tribole and Resch's main tenets in *Intuitive Eating* is to eat for physical reasons. It's tempting to turn this into a reworking of the calories in / calories out argument – that is, to turn intuitive eating into yet another diet. On bad days I berate myself for not recognising when I am full, or for picking up a chocolate bar for its soothing sweetness instead of confronting how I'm feeling: *that's not a physical reason to eat; you're doing it wrong*. Bad body, bad brain. It feels a lot like diet thinking, and I try to remember that other intuitive eating tenet: 'Reject the diet mentality'.

Even the new ways have their holes. The thing I patchwork together in order to be okay borrows, and borrows, and borrows, and is still incomplete.

—

Steven Poole, author of the satirical work *You Aren't What You Eat: Fed up with gastroculture*, articulates his frustration at popular memoirist Elizabeth Gilbert's glorification of self-sufficiency. He quotes a passage of her prose, in which Gilbert arranges a simple plate of food and is satisfied with its honesty. Poole suggests that those he calls *foodists* 'kneel in drooling awe before this portrait of a solipsist goddess miracling her own sustenance from thin air, thus demonstrating perfect dominion not only over other people but over the laws of nature themselves' – he's calling Gilbert a self-righteous wanker, really, and those who find her attitude to her own cooking appealing, self-righteous wankers also.

But self-sufficiency isn't about self-righteousness, and it isn't about what Poole calls 'supernatural artisanship'. It might be about powers of transformation and insight. It might be about the empowerment that results from being able to bring ingredients together with a sense of hope, possibility and honesty about what these things could *become*. It's optimism toward growth, and satisfaction with the humble. It's showing up for the thing that shows up for you: the reliability of what will happen when you put particular ingredients together in particular conditions. After a lifetime of being told you're not enough (or rather, that you're *too much* – and that shrinking the body is the pathway to salvation and happiness), it's so liberating to know that *you* can be the source of enough.

—

Comfort has no divide between 'good foods' and 'bad foods', just following what's enjoyable, recognising that it's what you want and need, and sometimes (or perhaps always; how to tell?) there's no difference between those two things.

Comfort is gravitating towards brown foods, which seem to be the richest, the most nostalgic, and the stodgiest, their solidity a part of their comfort. Comfort is the reminder that some things taste so good that they appear in iterations all over the globe: donuts, barbecue (both primarily brown), gravy.

When my life feels beyond my control, I know that I can rely on stock to reduce around garlic, thyme, and shallots, to make something thick and robust. I recognise how soothing flavour can be, and what a tonic it is for whatever is wrong.

A recent podcast called *The Habitat* documented an experimental simulation of life on Mars: six volunteers are placed in close quarters inside a dome in an uninhabited part of Hawaii. While living here, they execute all the actions expected of astronauts on Mars proper: they eat space food, they only go outside with full space gear, they conduct exploratory expeditions. NASA watches all of this, and measures the interpersonal dynamics – this experiment is testing for human nature, trying to ascertain the kinds (and combinations) of people who could withstand such a mission if or when it actually happens.

In episode five of the radio documentary, the crew 'gets pissed'. What started as a charming Sunday tradition of one crew member cooking breakfast burritos and shouting 'TORTILLA!' each time he throws one in a pan is now grating on everyone's nerves. They're angry, because in such cramped living conditions the strangest things become disconcerting. Meanwhile, the crew doctor records a personal log about how upset she is that people keep ordering comfort foods (like Cheetos and Oreos) from home in their resupply packages, rather than more nutritionally sound staples.

I imagine how the real astronauts might yearn after their comfort foods. There's something poetic and desperate about being as far as you can possibly be from home, and the comfort that can be gained from a familiar meal. Surrounded by reddish brown rubble of dirt and inhospitable air; cramped together with people, some of whom you might not like or always get along with; executing everyday tasks in ways that look entirely different to how they're done at home. For those who eventually do land on Mars, Earth will appear in its sky as a bright but still overwhelmingly distant star. In these circumstances, a bag of chips might become a lifeline: the only familiar thing in a strange new world.

—

MFK Fisher's food memoir, *The Gastronomical Me*, is punctuated with chapters titled 'The measure of my powers'. In these chapter titles, Fisher is referencing George Santayana's thought, that 'To be happy you must have taken the measure of your powers, tasted the fruits of your passion, and learned your place in the world'. These chapters of Fisher's document her progress towards self-sufficiency – her satisfaction with what she can provide for herself; her ability to satisfy her many hungers – bodily and not – through cooking and eating. Upon re-reading, I realise that Fisher's 'power' chapters reflect on people in her life – mostly women – who have cooked for her. Her own powers are measured using the benchmarks set by her childhood cook, her boarding-house Madame, her uncle. They demonstrate for Fisher what it is to be confident, and economical, and joyous in the kitchen. She learns how to create these things by and for herself, and how to nurture those around her with them.

There is power in understanding your appetites. The same with your hungers, and the places where the two meet. The measure of my powers is to recognise that this is power at all.

—

Food is where I go for comfort. Food is returning to myself – through food, I can remember what my body enjoys. Through food, I return home.

Even though I'm an adult, and even though the houses I grew up in are too far away, and inhabited by strangers, food is my way back. When I'm feeling sad or uncertain, food settles me. It sits warm and solid in my belly; it fuels my body and my brain. It gives me a way to share with people I love – it gives me a way to show them I care.

When none of this is being said, but I need to hear it, I go back to the foods my family has shared and the flavours that were there. Scrabbling back to the past, the best I can do to recreate those feelings is to eat, and let food be my comfort.

37

I have spent such a long time mourning my body shape, but it's not all there is.

In yoga I find strength and respite from my constantly ticking mind. I take comfort from the way that yoga has names for the strength that resides in my body: mountain pose, warrior pose, volcano pose, cobra pose. In the next-day pains as I walk through the world, I am soothed. My body is capable, my body is learning, my body is adaptive. My body bounces back. My body speaks, and I am training my ear to listen.

Much of modern yoga has strayed from its spiritual origins, and there's a booming yoga business where Sanskrit is thrown around casually for the benefit of white women in designer athleisure wear. In the body liberation space, I have found yoga teachers – both in person and online – who make yoga accessible to larger bodies. They do their best to decolonise the practice, recognising origins and steering as far as they can from the capitalist version of yoga that focuses on perfecting shapes, owning the right gear, and torturing the body. Practising with body-positive yoga teachers like Sarah Harry, Amber Karnes, Jessamyn Stanley and Dana Falsetti introduces a version of this body movement that is simply about listening, noticing, and responding with kindness and compassion.

The teacher who has made her way with most regularity into my life is Adriene Mishler. Through the power of the internet, she's been welcomed into many homes – at the time of writing, her YouTube channel (only one platform for her yoga videos) has over six million subscribers. She moves playfully, encouraging exploration of body space and mindful awareness. She speaks softly, and includes her dog Benji in each practice. She makes gentle jokes. She extends a tender invitation, and asks you only to go to the edges of where you're comfortable – noticing what they look like, and how maybe they're different on each side of your body, or on different days. While Mishler's online community and its real-world spin-offs are a successful business venture, they've also been a powerful healing tool for me and many like me who are approaching their own bodies like they would a stranger. Cautious, slow, curious.

Trauma researcher and psychiatrist Bessel van der Kolk has written about the ways that the body holds memory, trauma and emotion in his groundbreaking book *The Body Keeps the Score*. In it, he says: 'One of the clearest lessons from contemporary neuroscience is that our sense of ourselves is anchored in a vital connection with our bodies'. He goes on:

> In yoga you focus your attention on your breathing and on your sensations moment to moment. You begin to notice the connection between your emotions and your body – perhaps how anxiety about doing a pose actually throws you off balance. You begin to experiment with

changing the way you feel. Will taking a deep breath relieve that tension in your shoulder? Will focusing on your exhalations produce a sense of calm? [...] Trauma makes you feel as if you are stuck forever in a helpless state of horror. In yoga you learn that sensations rise to a peak and then fall.

I want to apologise to my body. Yes, for treating it badly – for the ways I've stretched it and punished it and denied it, but more because even when I did all those things I continued to hate it. Because treating it as badly as I possibly could, I still couldn't see it as enough. I got to the end of that road – knees buckling, heart breaking – and still thought my body did nothing for me; still believed it didn't serve me. I want to apologise because I couldn't see just what it *can* do and just how capably it carries me though the world ... I'm sorry, body. I'm sorry.

I want to pick up all my apologies and pile them on to the scales for measuring – what is this regret worth? How much does it weigh?

But I refuse to quantify any more – there's no love in that. I want to balance on my feet, rather than on scales.

I insist on striking a balance on my own terms.

38

My mum is a patchworker. She engages in the funny business of cutting shapes out of whole pieces of fabric, and then sewing them back together in new ways. The effects of this are utterly strange, striking even. The juxtaposition of patterns and colours create new ways of seeing – in wholes, not pieces. Meaning comes from stepping back. The 'tumbling blocks' pattern places light and dark diamonds at particular angles and in particular sequences, tricking the eye to see the flat quilt as something with extra dimensions, cubes jutting out all over it.

This sewing work is like my writing work – we pick perfectly good whole things apart and then put them back together again. It's not until they're back together in this new way that the improvement becomes visible – that they weren't perfectly good to begin with at all.

Here is my body – I have strewn it all over, thoroughly dissected and examined its pieces. I have put it back together again. It now looks – and I don't quite know whether this is just a trick of perspective – like there's more to it. It has dimensions I'd never noticed before. A new picture has formed when I juxtapose this with that. And I have reassembled a body I'm happier with now than when I began. It's the same body, but I understand it more. I feel more kindly towards it. I'm aware of what I put into it, when, and with whom, but this is no longer a form of punishment.

But then there's the lived reality of existing in a body that has actually been patchworked, as Dad's body has: cut apart, rearranged, stitched. Renegotiated. Our bodies are incredible, resilient things. They're not machines; they're more adaptive than that. Just like in Dad's cooking, where he tells me not to worry about measurements, and to just do what looks and feels right. We just recreate a body that serves our needs. That feels right. Without judgement, without worrying too much about what it means.

Pieces and wholes: perhaps that's what I've inherited from my family. I am grateful for the skill.

39

I'm no longer waiting for a better body. I have stopped putting things off until I am thinner or more confident. I am not waiting until I'm more worthy, because what if I never am? Some days I hate my body; some days things with food are still not working. In response to this, showing up daily to heal the body and my relationship with food becomes a prayer.

The body is an instrument, with its own grand symphonies and concertos.

The body sings. Crescendo. Diminuendo.

Hush – and listen.

—

I keep thinking I'd like another tattoo. There is one on my arm already. Around my twenty-first birthday, I got a black-and-white fountain pen dropping a patch of ink. Now it is a little smudged and warped, and I curse my body's movement for changing what was perfect when it was first applied. I want another tattoo, but know that my body isn't good enough for one. I try to smooth my skin with various lotions and creams, to make it perfect enough to appreciate, to make it worth decorating. I think that when I have body parts I find acceptable, *then* I'll cover them in things I like.

By the time the one-year anniversary of Opa's death comes around, I have stopped waiting for my perfect body to arrive. I make an appointment at a tattoo studio with an artist I admire, and she creates a beautiful design for me. I prop up on my side with a bundle of paper towel encased in cling wrap lifting my left leg up off the bed. Black, and green, and orange. Some yellow. Some purple. She uses surprising colours that don't seem to belong, but that make the design real.

This is a watercolour tattoo, and the artist doubles back over patches of colour several times to create the washed-out gradient. There is a sharp pain for a few seconds, before the flow of endorphins dampens it. The pain becomes a background fact – I am in my body, putting something beautiful permanently on it. This moment right here; this moment is real and immovable and I can be nowhere else, in no other body but my own. I am glad to be in it.

Less than an hour later I hug the tattooist before leaving the shop with cling wrap taped around my calf, covering a vivid watercolour sketch of a Dutch carrot.

—

The massage therapist presses tiny rivulets along my muscles. There is a subtle wave to her touch, as though her heartbeat is moving through her body and into mine. Pressure at a certain point on my shoulder blade creates a twitch in my upper arm. We pulse together.

Changing rhythm: the long, broad strokes across my shoulders, and the nuance of minute movement at the base of my skull, where I store all my tension. She moves my head in an impossibly small figure eight, and I feel the muscles shift below her fingers. Occasionally a sound from her body (a sniff, air moving somewhere between her stomach and her throat, a cough) makes me aware of the closeness and honesty of having one body tend to another in this way.

The impulse is to push back against massage. She takes my arm in her hands and presses against it, moves it so that the joint rotates in its socket. It's difficult to let this happen – it feels as though somebody else is driving my body – but I learn eventually to view the sensation with curiosity. My arm becomes both mine and hers, and we work on it together. I work to surrender, and she works to touch the sore and tender places. There is some pain in this body kindness.

It hurts to want so badly to crawl out of my body while someone works to keep me in it. She reads my body in detail, as though it's written in braille beneath my skin; as though it has something to say worth reading, and I begin to believe it too.

—

Memory lives inside the body and outside of it. It lives in things, and the body is sometimes just such a thing. Sometimes bodily memory is held in the world of objects, or of landscapes, or of rooms or dresses or songs or tattoos.

Marianne Hirsch unpacks WG Sebald's novel *Austerlitz*. Of its memory-seeking lead characters, she says, 'For them, the past is located in objects, images, and documents, in fragments and traces barely noticeable in the layered train stations, streets, and official and private buildings of the European cities in which they meet and talk'.

This observation of the places where memory lives reminds me of a tweet popular philosopher Alain de Botton made in 2012, which has since been deleted but which I documented because of the deep impression it made on me. In it, he said, 'Most of our childhood is stored not in photos, but in certain biscuits, lights of day, smells, textures of carpet.'

There is a surprising *thing*ness of memory. This is where it lives: here, and here, and here.

—

In writing my body, I have charted its re-writing, too. There is a body of text, but there is also the other thing – the text of the body. The breath and the *now.now.now.now* of the body is a poem, though not always a good one. The body is a story. The lived body is inscribed.

Here are the scars, here are the stretch marks. Here are the decorations I have chosen: a barbell, tunnels, ink.

In Kafka's story 'In the Penal Colony', a prisoner is punished by being placed under a harrow, with spikes that descend as the prisoner lies naked on a bed. 'The condemned man has to have the law he has transgressed inscribed by the harrow on his body.' This is how I think of the whole story of food: the good and the bad. The unspoken, the unshakable stories that surround us are pressed into our bodies, and each person lives with the indelible knowledge of what's expected. In my scars and stretch marks are my transgressions. My body also carries my protests, where I have tried to push back by changing its shape, or by turning my body inward against itself in acts of self-harm. Or the newer protests: the piercings and tattoos. All these things feel as obvious as if Kafka's machine had been at work on me.

Sense memories seem ideal for mapping: they have texture, and rhythm, and length. There is a topography of sense memory, and this is also written on the body. Invisible from the outside, but undeniable, too. I know where my memories live, and I am always finding new ones. When the reading of bodily inscription is punishment, this is a map of hurt. Mountains and valleys and unexpected rivers of *ouch*. But these maps can be read with curiosity, too. The noticing and mindful tending to the body honours everywhere that memories live. I find them still tucked into me all over. Sometimes they're good memories, and sometimes they're not. My body knows all of them.

Paying close attention like this helps me recognise that I love things that smell sweet and mellow – my favourite is lavender and tonka. My body switches on when I allow taste to be just one of my important senses. Each night when I go to bed, I rub this calming scent into my body, and greet all the parts I have made peace with, as well as those I hope one day to forgive and allow. I know there's a chance I won't – that recovery is incomplete and imperfect. This is my body. Not my mother's or my father's. Not the body I'm encouraged to have by the media and diet culture. This is the body I've treated harshly, the body I've punished, but also the body that has carried me around the world, and that has let me make the world a part of it.

Becoming reacquainted with my body – with what it needs and wants, with its shape and size, with what it feels like when satisfied or joyous or distressed or calm or sad – has been a process of recognising the togetherness and separation of bodies. The sameness and singularity of them.

Further Reading & Resources

The resources that follow had a big impact on my understanding of what's in this work – some in a peripheral way, some in a way that is more explicit. It's not an exhaustive bibliography, but a tasting plate of the important ideas that influenced this work and my thinking in it.

Mine is one story – there are so many more. My own thinking has been informed deeply by the hard work of marginalised and groundbreaking writers, researchers, and activists. Without them, their strength, and their insistence, I never would have written the book you now hold in your hands. I can't thank them enough. I hope that the reading and resources that follow provide some insight into the many stories and resources that are out there, and I truly hope that you'll seek them out.

Food
Brillat-Savarin, JA (2009). *The Physiology of Taste: Or meditations on transcendental gastronomy* (MFK Fisher, trans.). Knopf Doubleday Publishing Group, New York.

Fisher, MFK (1989). *The Gastronomical Me*. North Point Press, San Francisco.

Hage, G (1997). 'At home in the entrails of the west: Multiculturalism, ethnic food and migrant home-building'. In Grace, Hage, Johnson, Langsworth and Symonds, *Home/world: Space, community and marginality in Sydney's west* (pp. 99–153). Pluto Press.

Pollan, M (2009). *In Defense of Food: An eater's manifesto* (1st edition). Penguin Books UK, London.

Schwartz, O (2015, September 1). 'Nervous eaters'. From the *Monthly* website: <www.themonthly.com.au/issue/2015/september/1441029600/oscar-schwartz/nervous-eaters>

Scott, R (2014). *Salad Days*. Penguin Books, Melbourne.

Shepherd, GM (2012). *Neurogastronomy: How the brain creates flavour and why it matters*. Columbia University Press, New York.

Tandoh, R (2018). *Eat Up! Food, appetite and eating what you want*. Serpent's Tail, London.

Troisi, JD, & Gabriel, S (2011). 'Chicken soup really is good for the soul: "Comfort food" fulfills the need to belong'. *Psychological Science*, 22(6), 747–753. <doi.org/10.1177/0956797611407931>

Wilson, B (2015). *First Bite: How we learn to eat*. Basic Books, New York.

Wood, C (2012). *Love and Hunger: Thoughts on the gift of food*. Allen & Unwin, Sydney.

Memory

Atkinson, M (2018). *Traumata*. University of Queensland Press, Brisbane.

Casey, ES (2000). *Remembering: A phenomenological study*. Indiana University Press, Bloomington.

Hirsch, M (2008). 'The generation of postmemory'. *Poetics Today*, 29(1), 103–128.

Holtzman, JD (2006). 'Food and memory'. *Annual Review of Anthropology*, 35(1), 361–378.

Kolk, BA V der (2015). *The Body Keeps the Score: Mind, brain and body in the transformation of trauma*. Penguin Books Ltd, New York.

Lazar, D (2008). 'An introduction to truth'. In D Lazar (ed.), *Truth in nonfiction: Essays* (pp. ix–xiii). University of Iowa Press, Iowa City.

Memory and Forgetting | Radiolab. (n.d.). From WNYC Studios website: <www.wnycstudios.org/podcasts/radiolab/episodes/91569-memory-and-forgetting>

Proust, M (2003). *In Search of Lost Time #1: Way by Swanns* (L Davis, trans.). Penguin Classic, London.

Sutton, DE (2001). *Remembrance of Repasts: An anthropology of food and memory*. Berg, Oxford; New York.

Verbeek, C, & van Campen, C (2013). 'Inhaling memories'. *The Senses and Society*, 8(2), 133–148.

Nondiet science

042: The Minnesota Starvation Experiment. (2016). From
Bacon, L (2010). *Health at Every Size: The surprising truth about your weight*
  (2nd edition). BenBella Books, Dallas.

Bacon, L, & Aphramor, L (2011). 'Weight science: Evaluating the evidence
  for a paradigm shift'. *Nutrition Journal*, 10, 9.

Bacon, L, & Aphramor, L (2014). *Body Respect: What conventional health
  books get wrong, leave out, and just plain fail to understand about weight*
  (1st edition). BenBella Books, Dallas.

Boothroyd, LG, Tovée, MJ, & Pollet, TV (2012). 'Visual diet versus
  associative learning as mechanisms of change in body size preferences
  (Mechanisms of change in body size preferences)'. PLoS ONE. 7(11).

Harrison, C (2019). *Anti-Diet: Reclaim your time, money, well-being, and
  happiness through intuitive eating*. Little, Brown Spark, New York.

Harrison, C (2013–2020). Food Psych Podcast. [Audio podcast]. From
  <christyharrison.com/foodpsych>

Heyes, CJ (2006). 'Foucault goes to Weight Watchers'. *Hypatia*, 21(2),
  126–149.

Hobbes, M (2018). 'Everything you know about obesity is wrong'. From the
  Huffington Post website: <highline.huffingtonpost.com/articles/en/
  everything-you-know-about-obesity-is-wrong/>

Kalm, LM, & Semba, RD (2005). 'They starved so that others be better
  fed: Remembering Ancel Keys and the Minnesota Experiment'. *The
  Journal of Nutrition*, 135(6), 1347–1352.

Orbach, S (2016). *Fat Is a Feminist Issue*. Arrow Books, London.

Polivy, J (1996). 'Psychological consequences of food restriction'. *Journal of
  the American Dietetic Association*, 96(6), 589–592.

Spiel, EC, Paxton, SJ, & Yager, Z (2012). 'Weight attitudes in 3- to 5-year-old
  children: Age differences and cross-sectional predictors'. *Body Image*,
  9(4), 524–527.

Tandoh, R (2016, May 14). 'The unhealthy truth behind "wellness" and
  "clean eating"'. From *Vice* website: <www.vice.com/en_au/article/
  jm5nvp/ruby-tandoh-eat-clean-wellness>

Tribole, E (2012). *Intuitive Eating: A revolutionary program that works*
  (3rd edition). St. Martin's Griffin, New York.

Wilson, B (2016). *This Is Not a Diet Book: A user's guide to eating well*.
  Fourth Estate, London.

Wilson, B (2017). 'Why we fell for clean eating'. From the *Guardian* website:
  <www.theguardian.com/lifeandstyle/2017/aug/11/why-we-fell-for-
  clean-eating>

Body writing and representation

Brien, DL (2013). 'Starving, bingeing and writing: Reading and writing memoirs of eating disorder'. *TEXT Special Issue: Nonfiction Now*, (18).

Enders, G (2017). *Gut: New revised and expanded edition* (B format edition). Scribe Publications, Melbourne.

Keys, A (1950). *The Biology of Human Starvation: Volume I*. The University of Minnesota Press, Minneapolis.

Kirkby, T & Caron, B (Directors) (2013–2015). *My Mad Fat Diary*. [Television series]. E4, London.

Loughman, A, Jackson, M, & Bertrand, P (n.d.). 'Gut feeling: How your microbiota affects your mood, sleep and stress levels'. From the *Conversation* website: <theconversation.com/gut-feeling-how-your-microbiota-affects-your-mood-sleep-and-stress-levels-65107>

Taylor, SR (2018). *The Body Is Not an Apology: The power of radical self-love* (1st edition). Berrett-Koehler Publishers, Oakland.

Walker, S (2015). *Dietland*. Nero, Collingwood.

West, L (2016). *Shrill: Notes from a loud woman*. Hachette UK, London.

Wright, F (2015). *Small Acts of Disappearance*. Giramondo Publishing, Sydney.

Zimmerman, J (2016). 'Hunger Makes Me'. From *Hazlitt* website: <hazlitt.net/feature/hunger-makes-me>

Support services

The Butterfly Foundation: 1800 33 4673
HAES Australia lists nondiet and weight-neutral practitioners on its website:
Lifeline: 13 11 14
   6pm–midnight (AEST) crisis text: 0477 13 11 14
   <www.lifeline.org.au>
SANE Australia: 1800 18 7263
   <www.sane.org>

Acknowledgments

Writing a book is a collaborative endeavour, and there are many people to whom I'm so grateful for their patience across years as I agonised over the creation of this book. They each, in their own way, kept me upright (or helped it be okay when I collapsed), and insisted that this story needed to be ushered into the world – without them, the book you hold would not exist.

Thanks to Faber and Faber Ltd for permission to quote Seamus Heaney's 'When all the others were away at Mass' ('*from* Clearances').

The value of institutional support can't be underestimated. Financial security, space to write, and support in the form of publication – these things all tell a writer that their work is valuable and has an audience. I'm grateful to those who published sections of this book in various forms on the Wheeler Centre's 'Notes', in *Kill Your Darlings*, and in *Jumble*. Thanks to Express Media and Scribe for shortlisting an early version of this project for the 2015 Scribe Nonfiction Prize.

Thanks to *Kill Your Darlings* and their Unpublished Manuscript Award, which provided professional development and a valuable platform. I was so lucky to receive a

Kill Your Darlings/Varuna Copyright Agency Fellowship, which gave me time and space to focus on structure and voice. Thanks to Rebecca, and to Shelley, Matt and Lisa. And, of course, the Varuna staff – especially chef extraordinaire Sheila, who kept my body going while my mind was elsewhere.

Thanks to the Wheeler Centre and the Readings Foundation for a Hot Desk Fellowship, which took the work from a long essay to a real, proper manuscript, and gave the work its first public audience.

Thanks to NonfictioNOW for allowing me to speak about my research and project, and to the Melbourne City of Literature Office for funding my trip to the USA to attend the 2015 conference.

Thanks to David Carlin, whose interest in the tension of this story was what encouraged me to keep leaning toward the discomfort in the first place. Thanks to the late Adrian Miles, whose research methods have taught me how to pace myself, how to work hard, and how to finish things. Thanks to Brigid Magner and my Honours cohort in the Consilience Lab at RMIT. Thanks to the RMIT non/fictionLab, which provided me space to write at the Urban Writing House, where I was able to cut the text up, shuffle it around and see it differently.

Thanks to Fiona Wright, for mentoring and seriously engaging with something so protean. You buoyed my spirits when I was ready to throw it all in by telling me that 'straightforward is for chumps, and so is risklessness'. Thanks to Rebecca Giggs for cheerleading, checking in, and giving so much when she absolutely didn't have to.

To the team at NewSouth: thanks to Harriet McInerney for taking a chance and for believing this was worth advocating for. For recognising what this is, and never asking it to be anything else. Thanks to Jocelyn Hungerford for precise, safe, and kind copyedits. Thanks to Paul O'Beirne for overseeing this project so capably.

Thanks to Son Nair, Kylie Maslen, and Ronnie Sullivan for their generous feedback and patience, and to Lou Omer for her moral support. Our regular writing group validated this story, and gave it space to grow. Thanks for insisting I read *Shrill*, for letting me cry, for always believing that this story would find its place, and that it's going to be useful to others. Thanks for always seeking out the hash browns with me, even during the great Melbourne hash brown downturn of 2016. You're all brilliant.

Thanks to Katie Found, Pepi Ronalds, and the Athenaeum Library (and her keepers) for keeping me coming back to rework.

Thanks to Chloe Papas for being my wing woman and speculative real estate partner – I can't wait for the witchy house. Thanks to Stefi Markidis for helping slay the dragon. Thanks to Connor O'Brien for always asking, encouraging and validating. Thanks to T+N+Z+S, for the baby photos, the accommodation, the endless curiosity and support. Thanks to Laurie Steed for having supported and mentored me with great empathy from the very start.

To my team of carers, who made all the difference by giving me access to outstanding and safe treatment, which is a huge privilege: Kathryn, Richard, Lou, and Elle.

To Mum, Dad, and Chris for your generosity in finding

space for me to write this, and for always caring for me. To my extended family: van Zwedens, Buises, Bonnicis, Sonegos, Pressers, and Levys.

And finally, to Danny, for holding space for me to live and write my truth, and for meeting me there. Your willingness to stand and grow alongside me, even when the way forward looks scary or uncertain, are qualities I treasure and love so much about you. To you and Phoebe, for being the family I'm so lucky to come home to every day.